The Astrology of Development

Stephanie Jean Clement

Copyright 2007 Stephanie Jean Clement
All rights reserved

No part of this book may be reproduced or transcribed in any form or by any means, electronic or mechanical, including photocopying or recording or by any information storage and retrieval system without written permission from the author and publisher, except in the case of brief quotations embodied in critical reviews and articles. Requests and inquiries may be mailed to: American Federation of Astrologers, Inc., 6535 S. Rural Road, Tempe, AZ 85283.

ISBN-10: 0-86690-596-0
ISBN-13: 978-0-86690-596-1

Cover Design: Jack Cipolla

Published by:
American Federation of Astrologers, Inc.
6535 S. Rural Road
Tempe, AZ 85283

www.astrologers.com

Printed in the United States of America

Dedication

**To Greg
Terry and Shelly
Lynda and Leonard
Tatsuo, Ivy, Katherine, and Genavieve**

Acknowledgments

First, many thanks to Noel Tyl for his generous assistance
with the manuscript, and for his foreword.

Thanks to Cosmic Patterns Software, Esoteric Technologies, Matrix Software, and Intrepid
Software for the powerful tools they have provided to astrologers.

Thanks to Stuart Farrel, whose encouragement and suggestions were so very valuable.

And thanks to Georgia Stathis for impressing on me the importance of lunar phases.

Contents

Foreword by Noel Tyl

Introduction, Planetary Cycles You May Have Overlooked

Chapter One, Astrology and Human Development   1

Chapter Two, Planetary Aspect Cycles and Retrogrades   5

Chapter Three, The Moon   21

Chapter Four, The Sun, Mercury, and Venus   35

Chapter Five, Mars   49

Chapter Six, Jupiter   59

Chapter Seven, Saturn   69

Chapter Eight, Uranus   81

Chapter Nine, Neptune   91

Chapter Ten, Pluto   102

Appendix One, Planetary Cycles from Birth Date: Age Index   115

Appendix Two, Pluto Ingresses to Signs   127

Bibliography   133

List of Charts and Illustrations

Illustration
Chapter Ten
    Pluto Graph

Astrological Charts
Chapter Two
    Donald Trump
    Charles Darwin
    Male 1
    Male 2
Chapter Three
    Arthur Young Birth Chart
    Phase Angle Chart April 29, 1944
Chapter Four
    Oprah Winfrey
    J. Paul Getty
Chapter Five
    Katarina Witt
    Debi Thomas
Chapter Six
    Louis Armstrong
    Donald Trump (repeat)
Chapter Eight
    His Holines, the Karmapa
Chapter Nine
    William Butler Yeats
    Kurt Cobain
    Elizabeth Taylor
Chapter Ten
    Olga Korbut
    Nadia Comaneci
    John Roberts
    Benjamin Franklin

Foreword

Every astrology student learns first off that the microcosm—the organized systemology of our being—reflects the macrocosm—the organization of our solar system. We learn that what is below is so because of what is above. This observation links everything we know in parallelisms that are dramatically integrated.

The microcosm-macrocosm concept refers as well to *time*. Our subjective development in life reflects the objective demarcation of time, and vice versa. We are what we are when we are supposed to be. Our astrology marks these passages.

Every astrology student also learns with wonder the drama of planetary cycles within time: how a transiting planet returning to its natal position, i.e., one complete orbit around the individual Sun, says something, en route and upon completion, and upon commencement of yet another cycle. This is the heart of astrological thinking—the organization of time reflected in cycles of development.

Stephanie Jean Clement has taken this path to insight further than any astrologer in the literature so far: she inspects *the first unit of motion*—that first orbit of a planet to its natal position within the emerging time of life development—and establishes *the imprint of lifelong propensity and vulnerability*. Macro-time contains micro-development, and the planetary motions show that.

In the process, Clement so clearly revives the all-too-easily forgotten dictum, the classic teaching that no event will occur that cannot be foreseen in the natal horoscope.

This dictum is intriguing indeed, almost mystical, but it is frustrating at the same time; every astrological generation finds it so. The reason is that we do not know easily where to find "everything" in the horoscope. Some of us can go further than others, but in our lifelong study of life we all pull up short too often. Clement zeroes in on the heretofore elusive motion measurements of the initial planetary cycle in an individual's life and shows dramatically that the subtle phase measurements of that initial motion set the tone for all future development in terms of the respective planet.

There is a dramatic case of two people injured severely in an auto accident, and how each suffered injuries reflected clearly in the first-orbit time-development period after their birth, different for each individual. The "difference" has to do with the date of birth, the speedy initial orbit of the individual Moon, the to-and-fro of Mercury and Venus in the time of their first orbit, the vitality measures of Mars, etc.

In Clement's study, we see new life and reason given to so-called minor aspects like the semisextile, the semisquare and others. These are marks of passage of keen significance within the first orbit of each planet after one's birth.

Clement extends the micro-measurement of macro cycles to invigorate secondary progressions. The first-orbit progressed measurements of Mercury and Venus articulate most persuasively lifelong significances from initial-orbit retrogradation periods!

We see how premature births will "upset" the timing of events in later life, requiring months or even years for the young organism to "catch up" within the system. And this imprint is lifelong in occurrence! It fascinates me how Clement's acutely sensitive insights to earliest growth actually reflect cultural wisdoms that have been organized over so many centuries of observation and instinctive knowing. The astrology vividly frames all that for reliable reference.

A natural outgrowth of this specialized study introduces phase angles (the Sun-Moon phase angle is fundamental to the heretofore much heralded Jonas method of astrological birth control and gender selection). It introduces refreshed consideration and significance for planetary return charts! Clement says that throughout the entire life, we can notice certain themes coming up again and again and again. Now, we know where to look to find these signals.

This fine, fine study stimulates growth for any thinking astrologer. Although I am living within my third Saturn cycle—fully aware of the portents of that long first cycle and the wiser second cycle—I still was touched and illuminated by Clement's insights for this third cycle. I was rewarded to see how my initial, swift Mercury cycle set up my mind for the Saturn architecture to come; how it is still working now.

This is happening for you too in your individual portion of time. Follow Clement's thoughts and very clear age-reference numbers; capture the phase sensibility within the Microcosm reflection of the Macro-Order. You will be much the richer for it; much the wiser; and grateful to Stephanie Clement for showing from whence we came.

Noel Tyl
Fountain Hills, AZ
October 2006

Introduction

Planetary Cycles You May Have Overlooked

Each planet's unique cycle reflects human developmental processes aside from the impact of interplanetary aspects and patterns. We observe the Moon's transits in the sky every month, and our calendars even mark the New, Quarter, and Full Moons. The cycle of the Moon is used heavily in horary astrology, and its movement marks one of the central considerations in secondary progressions. The news here is that each of the planets has a similar cycle, and we can track planetary transits in relationship to their birth positions. These transits account for almost every significant developmental step from birth to old age.

In actuality, the aspects of a planet from birth until its first return are the most powerful. All subsequent returns and aspects reflect the nature of the first cycle. As you consider each planet in this book, you will see the immense significance of retrograde periods. Retrogrades during the first year of life describe our earliest developmental process. Retrograde Venus or Mars, for example, can indicate a substantial deviation from the normal social and physical developmental timing associated with these two planets. The differences are even more striking in secondary progressions, where the initial transits are projected over the rest of our lives, marking periods of consolidation or regressive tendencies, or times when we are retracing our steps, just as we did in infancy. The childhood experiences of each transit and return set us up for a lifetime of physical, emotional, and mental habits.

Every stage of development from birth to adulthood and old age is strongly marked by the initial cycles of the Moon, Sun and planets. Except for the outer planets, most people experience the returns of the planets to their birth position. The first of each of these returns, along with the aspects formed along the way, are powerful indicators of developmental challenges.

Astrologers sometimes make the mistake of thinking that each time a planet reaches a square, opposition or conjunction to its birth position, one can expect equally powerful events. This is simply not the case. We learn from the personal experience of each transit, and thus we modify, amplify, or ameliorate the effects of subsequent transits. For example, the Moon has formed a conjunction with your birth Moon hundreds of times during your life. Aside from all other indications, the first transit at about age twenty-seven days was the most profound indicator of the Moon's effect on your physical, mental, emotional and spiritual development. Hundreds of transits later you are still affected by Moon conjunction Moon, but you have a storehouse of experience that allows you to work with the energy instead of against it. The same is true for all the planets, with their corresponding longer return periods and fewer transits, down to Neptune and Pluto, which will never make a complete transit of your chart.

By following the movement of the planets and observing the interweaving of planetary energies, we can map development clearly. We can observe the independent actions of each planet as markers for developmental processes that occur for all of us at approximately the same age. Based on what we observe about the first return of each planet to its birth position, we can develop suggestions for how to deal with later repetitions more effectively.

Basics of Child Development

One simple method of understanding child development involves allowing two and one half years for each sign, beginning with Aries, even when the child is not an Aries. This means that all children, regardless of their Sun signs, display Aries qualities during the first two and one half years of life, Taurus qualities in the second two and one-half years, and so on. By age thirty, each individual has experienced an infusion of the structured qualities of each sign; this timing corresponds to Saturn's transit around the chart.

Throughout the book we will examine physical, mental, emotional, and spiritual developmental processes that carry us from birth to death and perhaps beyond. Consider the idea that babies have unique temperaments even before they are born. Ask any mother of more than one child and she will tell you she knew the difference before delivery.

Astrology is quite good at delineating temperament. Some measures work very well in infancy, while others work better after the child can talk well. Still other indications only occur much later, when the outer planets have had time to move through the birth chart. You can compare a planet's unique developmental markers with transiting aspects among two or more planets to identify significant moments in people's lives. Taken together, these two factors—a planet's aspects to itself and aspects between planets—indicate developmental rhythms unique to each individual.

A third indicator is the social milieu in which we live. Astrology provides powerful indicators for development, but so do economic conditions, social and ethnic considerations, and nuclear family composition and function. Thus we must evaluate astrological considerations against the background of an individual's physical, mental, emotional and spiritual life conditions. If you are born into a wealthy situation, massive resources can be mobilized to help you develop budding sports, music or other talent. If your parents don't have an extra dime at the end of each month, your economic opportunities will be more limited.

For development in infancy, consider the transiting cycles of Sun, Mercury, Venus and Mars. The first three share an approximate one-year cycle, with Mars at approximately two years. Mercury has three retrograde periods each year, so it traverses significant portions of the zodiac three times in its annual dance (each time it retrogrades, it goes back about seventeen degrees before it turns to go forward again. Venus has a retrograde period approximately every eighteen months, and goes back about fifteen or sixteen degrees.

Depending on the rhythm of the retrogrades, the Sun, Mercury and Venus will reach their quarter phases before or after each other, even though they all transit the complete zodiac in about one year. In one person's chart, Mercury, the fastest planet of the three, will reach the quarter first, while in another chart Venus may be first. This occurs because of intervening retrograde periods. A more extreme instance occurs when transiting Venus reaches the closing trine (240 degrees) after Mars has reached the closing square (270 degrees)! This particular occurrence would denote a significant lag in social development behind the development of motor skills.

This book will describe the developmental challenges of each of the planets during its first cycle, along with the approximate age at which each will occur. In addition, it will look at the effect of retrograde periods on the developmental process. Then it will consider what happens when aspects of different planets occur out of the expected order because of retrograde cycles. Because the Jupiter and Saturn cycles mark major developmental challenges throughout adulthood, I will include information on the second and later cycles of these two planets. Uranus, Neptune, and Pluto also have developmental impact through a lifetime, but the human life span does not allow for us to experience a second, or even first, full cycle of these planets.

As you read about the various developmental challenges, keep in mind that almost everyone meets these challenges in a positive, constructive, creative way. Each of us is living proof that the human model is designed to meet challenges of all kinds and to master them. In fact, we all meet the initial challenges of life at very nearly the same time. Astrological factors like speed of the planets and retrograde periods define individual differences in the timing of many challenges as well as individual responses to them.

An additional caveat: If your child misses the developmental timing listed in this book, don't worry! The dates included here are averages, with considerable variation on both sides of the mark. For example, my son showed very little inclination to crawl for quite some time. I worried, and I asked his doctor about it. The doctor said he was growing very rapidly and that his body was simply too heavy for his muscles to bear the weight. Give him a week or two. Sure enough, he crawled "all at once," and was faster than I ever imagined possible! If you are in doubt about a developmental step, your pediatrician can check to make sure everything is "on schedule" with your baby.

Note: This book includes charts of individuals for whom we have no accurate birth times. The beauty of the developmental processes outlined in this book is that birth time is not a major factor. For the outer planets and the Sun, changes in birth time do not significantly impact the unfolding of the cycles. For Mercury, Venus, and Mars, the cycles can vary slightly if the planet happens to reach a stationary position within a day or two. For the Moon, the differences are slight as well. This may come as a surprise to some astrologers, yet it is true—*the methods described in this book work quite well even for unknown birth times*.

Throughout the book, secondary progression and solar arc aspects to the natal position are considered. We will also consider the phase angle between any pair of planets and the cycle through which this angle is repeated. For those who are unfamiliar with phase angles, you will find a definition in Chapter One, with a discussion of the Sun to Moon and Sun to Mars phase angle returns.

Finally, we will discuss the relationships among the planetary cycles and how they affect the so-called normal developmental process. For example, if several planetary indicators make aspects to their natal positions at the same time, this could indicate acceleration or delay of developmental processes.

Nothing in this book discounts the importance of interplanetary aspects. They play a dynamic role in natal delineation, forecasting, and chart comparison. However, interplanetary aspects are seldom considered in this book because the focus is on each planet's transits to its own position in the birth chart. The discussion here addresses the aspects of each planet to its own position up to the first planetary return, and also considers that retrogrades, secondary progressions, solar arcs, and phase angles will show how the initial pass of a planet is reflected later in life.

Chapter One

Astrology and Human Development

A birth chart indicates the powerful transits at work at the time an infant enters the world. The chart is a snapshot of planetary energies that have come together to reflect physical, emotional, mental and spiritual potential for the individual's life. As such, the chart indicates the strengths the individual has to begin with, and also shows the potential for future creative development. Developmental considerations depend on the birth chart. By this I mean that no event will occur that cannot be foreseen from the birth chart. This fact is often overlooked by students, and cannot be emphasized enough.

The nature of each planet, along with its aspects, reveals a picture of the environment surrounding the birth itself. Highly stressful charts sometimes indicate conditions at the time of birth that may cause delays or irregularities in development. However, the vast majority of infants weather challenges beautifully. Traditional astrology provides volumes of information about the possibilities for each infant.

Each planet has a specific role in development. As we look at the initial cycles of each of the planets, we can see the kinds of developmental challenges to be expected, as well as the strengths and weaknesses of the person. This book narrows the range of planetary meanings to deal with specific developmental processes. The cycles of the planets vary in length. Basically, the longer the cycle, the later in life a particular developmental demand is encountered and addressed.

The first full cycle of the Moon represents an essential period. Because the Moon's cycle is so short, the infant experiences every possible aspect of the Moon within one lunar month. All lunar aspects later in life are "replays" of the initial lunar aspects, with cycles of other planets providing complementary energies throughout the life.

Specific indicators in the birth chart relate to early childhood development. Each planet in the birth chart indicates developmental processes. Here are a few examples of planets paired with information from Jane Healy's book, *Your Child's Growing Mind*,[1] concerning neo-natal development:

- Neptune—Sleep and rest.
- Mercury and Saturn—Response to voices or other sounds.
- Uranus—The startle reflex and other reflexes.
- Mercury—Different crying sounds to communicate different moods or needs.
- Mercury, Gemini—Development of language within appropriate time limits.
- Venus, Libra, and Uranus—Symmetry (Venus) or asymmetry (Uranus) of limb movements is observed.
- Sun, Aries, or First House emphasis—Strong eye contact with parents.
- Venus—Social responsiveness, such as snuggling.
- Jupiter, Sun—These planets indicate growth or weight changes in general.

This short list shows a few astrological factors paired with developmental processes. As we consider the Moon, Sun, and each planet, an astrological developmental guide emerges. I have included a comprehensive developmental guide in Appendix One for reference purposes.

When you use the developmental tables, remember that the dates are averages, and not absolute deadlines!

Astrological Cycles

Once past the birth process and any initial crisis, we can use astrological cycles as a guide to developmental processes. In addition, each developmental milestone provides a metaphor for later development. As mentioned above, the lunar cycle gets the infant off to a quick start in life. The first few aspects of each planet to its birth position reflect the lunar cycle, and they amplify the planet's energy. The aspects of each planet mark the prominent points in each planet's cycle. In addition to the four dominant angles (opening square, opposition, closing square, and first conjunction of the planet to the natal position), we can also look at the twelfth harmonic (30 degree aspects), and the eighth harmonic (semisquare and sesquisquare) for additional information about a planet's relationship to its birth position.

This book focuses on three considerations:

- The aspect of a transiting planet to itself in the natal chart.
- The phase angle between two planets, meaning the angular distance in longitude between two natal planets.
- Stations and retrograde periods.

The phase angle return occurs when the two planets are the same distance apart by transit as they are in the natal chart. For example, the phase angle between the Moon and Sun is the same on June 1, June 30, and July 29, 2008. On each date the Sun is about 31 degrees ahead of the Moon in the zodiac.

Date	*Time*	*Sun Position*	*Moon Position*	*Separation*
June 1, 2008	Noon	11 Gemini 31	10 Taurus 58	30° 33'
June 30, 2008	3:21 pm	9 Cancer 28	8 Gemini 55	30° 33'
July 29, 2008	9:21 pm	7 Leo 23	6 Cancer 50	30° 33'

Note: When considering aspects between the natal Sun and transiting Moon, the Moon reaches the same aspect in about twenty-seven days, and the aspect occurs in the same signs as in the natal chart. Because the Sun is also moving when we consider the phase angle return, the intervals for phase angles are longer, and the signs change as well.

The angle between any two planets in a birth chart suggests a natural inclination regarding the interaction of the two planets' energies. The "phase angle return" reflects moments in a life when the birth potential is renewed along the same lines as in the birth chart. When a phase angle return occurs in signs different from those in the birth chart, a developmental shift is indicated.

To illustrate the phase angle of Sun to Mars, we find a Gemini-Leo relationship in the June 1, 2008 chart, a Cancer-Virgo relationship in the July 8, 2010 chart, and a Leo-Libra relationship in the August 17, 2012 chart.

Date	Time	Sun Position	Mars Position	Separation
June 1, 2008	Noon	11 Gemini 31	12 Leo 34	61° 04'
July 8, 2010	3:21 pm	16 Cancer 06	17 Virgo 09	61° 04'
August 17, 2012	10:36 am	25 Leo 12	26 Libra 15	61° 04'

The time intervals are approximately equal here, but they can vary somewhat, depending on the timing of retrograde periods of Mars. The periods are longer because the Sun and Mars move much slower than the Moon. The forward shift in development is reiterated.

In considering only the above two types of angles, we see the potential for tremendous complexity. A planet has a relationship to its own position and a phase relationship to every other planet in the chart. A planet also forms aspects by transit and progression, creating a staggering number of potential developmental milestones in a lifetime. This book focuses on the aspects of each planet to its own position. These aspects coincide with key points in physiological, mental, emotional, and spiritual development throughout the lifetime. The reader should keep in mind that an exploration of the phase angle returns of planetary pairs will reveal a great deal of additional data about individual development.

The following chapters of development examine the faster moving planets first. The book's primary focus is on a planet's first trip around the chart after birth. There is also information about progressed motion (especially for the Moon) and for angular relationships between the Sun and other planets. The interested reader may wish to consider other phase angle relationships in light of the meanings of aspects presented in the chapter on the Moon.

Chapter Two

Planetary Aspect Cycles and Retrogrades

There are a few points I wish to make throughout this book. They have major importance where human development in childhood and adulthood are concerned. I will reemphasize these points often. Some of these ideas will be obvious to most readers, yet they represent a new way of thinking about planetary cycles.

First: The first return of a planet in aspect its natal position is of far greater importance than subsequent transits. This is true in terms of physical and mental development in earliest childhood. It is also true of emotional and spiritual development on a life-long basis, given that many of us will never see a full cycle of Uranus, and none of us will live to see a full cycle of Neptune and Pluto (unless incredible medical breakthroughs occur!). The first time a planet reaches each of the aspects to its natal position marks a milestone.

Second: The events and conditions at each milestone, along with the mental, emotional, and spiritual impressions made by these events, set the tone for all future development. With some planets this fact will be obvious, and with other planets the impressions will be subtle. Nevertheless, the first phase cycle sets the tone, and changing that tone may require significant effort.

Third: The effort required to change the tone of the first cycle depends on several things:

- The nature of the events that occurred on the first transit
- The nature of the impressions that were made during the first transit
- The intensity of those impressions
- The degree to which those impressions were conscious, or can be recalled and reconsidered
- The individual's response to retrograde periods

Some examples will explain these points.

Suppose that on the first lunar transit, within the first month of life, the infant receives appropriate physical nourishment. There is an immediate impact on weight gain, and early physical and mental development. A tone of healthy nourishment has been struck, and there could be an accompanying tone of satisfying nurturance on the emotional level. In most cases the long-term effects are extremely subtle. Even though parents sometimes struggle with the initial problem of getting enough nourishment to the child, the problem is resolved and the infant begins to gain weight and develop normally in other ways. For the child, the first lunar cycle takes on personal meaning that translates into a monthly reflection of emotional challenges met with satisfactory future development.

On a grander scale, the aspects of the secondary progressed Moon and the solar arc Moon to the natal position will mark especially poignant reminders of the initial cycle. Therefore what occurred at about age two and one-half days of life will be reflected at about age two and one-half years by the secondary progressed Moon, and at about age thirty years by the solar arc Moon. What occurred at about age two weeks will be reflected at age fourteen or fifteen years by the secondary progressed Moon (the solar arc Moon will not reach this aspect during a normal life span). The same pattern is true for all the planets, with diminishing effect by secondary progression, and with the exact same effect by solar arc.

Because of their slow speed, the outer planet transits mingle in a dance with solar arcs. Here are listings of Pluto aspects to natal Pluto for Donald Trump and Charles Darwin.

To simplify the list, I have included only the first instance of each aspect and ignored retrograde and direct passes over the same degree. Note the solar arc aspects that will occur during Trump's life.

Transit and Solar Arc Pluto Aspects: Donald Trump

Event	Date	Aspect Type
Pluto semisextile Pluto	November 23, 1961	Transit
Pluto semisquare Pluto	December 11, 1968	Transit
Pluto sextile Pluto	October 26, 1975	Transit
Pluto semisextile Pluto	**November 26, 1977**	*Solar Arc*
Pluto square Pluto	December 6, 1987	Transit
Pluto semisquare Pluto	**August 9, 1993**	*Solar Arc*
Pluto trine Pluto	February 1, 1999	Transit
Pluto sesquisquare Pluto	January 5, 2006	Transit
Pluto sextile Pluto	**April 2, 2009**	*Solar Arc*
Pluto quincunx Pluto	January 21, 2013	Transit
Pluto opposition Pluto	March 29, 2029	Transit
Pluto square Pluto	**March 31, 2040**	*Solar Arc*

Note also that Donald Trump has no secondary progressed Pluto aspect to natal Pluto. The only possible progressed Pluto aspect is the conjunction, which occurs when natal Pluto changes direction shortly after birth, in which case progressed Pluto may conjunct natal Pluto.

Second, in this list of one hundred year's worth of Pluto aspects, there are four solar arc Pluto aspects. Because solar arc is quite uniform, everyone will experience the Pluto aspects close to the age when Donald Trump did.

Third, in this list there are eight transiting Pluto aspects to natal Pluto, not including retrograde passes. The eccentric orbit of Pluto assures us that people born with Pluto in different signs will experience these transiting aspects at very different ages. In the Pluto chapter, this variation in the cycles is explored in depth.

Now look at a comparable table for Charles Darwin, who was born at a time when Pluto was moving much more slowly.

8/The Astrology of Development

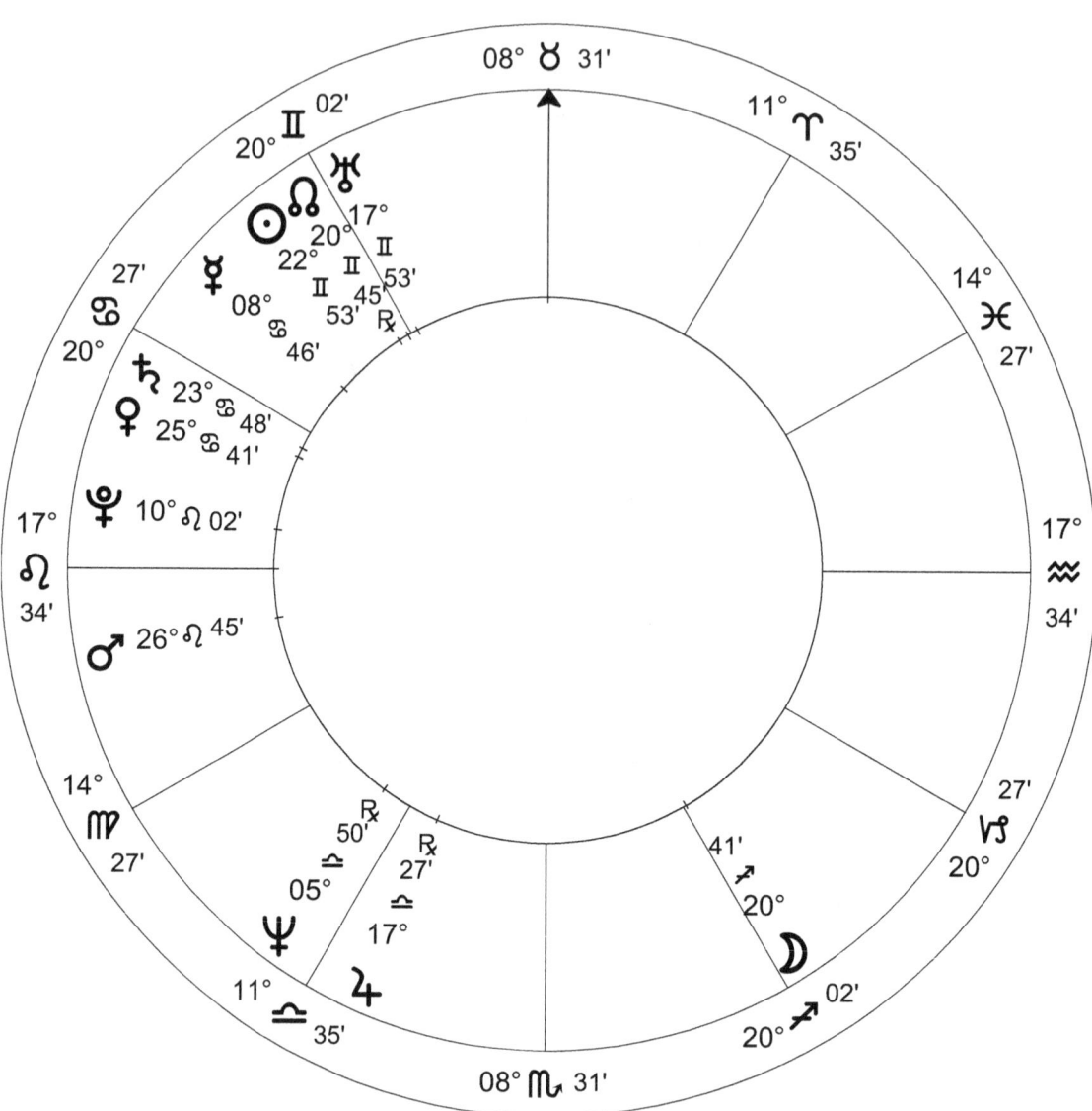

Donald Trump, June 14, 1946, 9:51 a.m., Queens, New York
Tropical, Koch

Planetary Aspect Cycles and Retrogrades/9

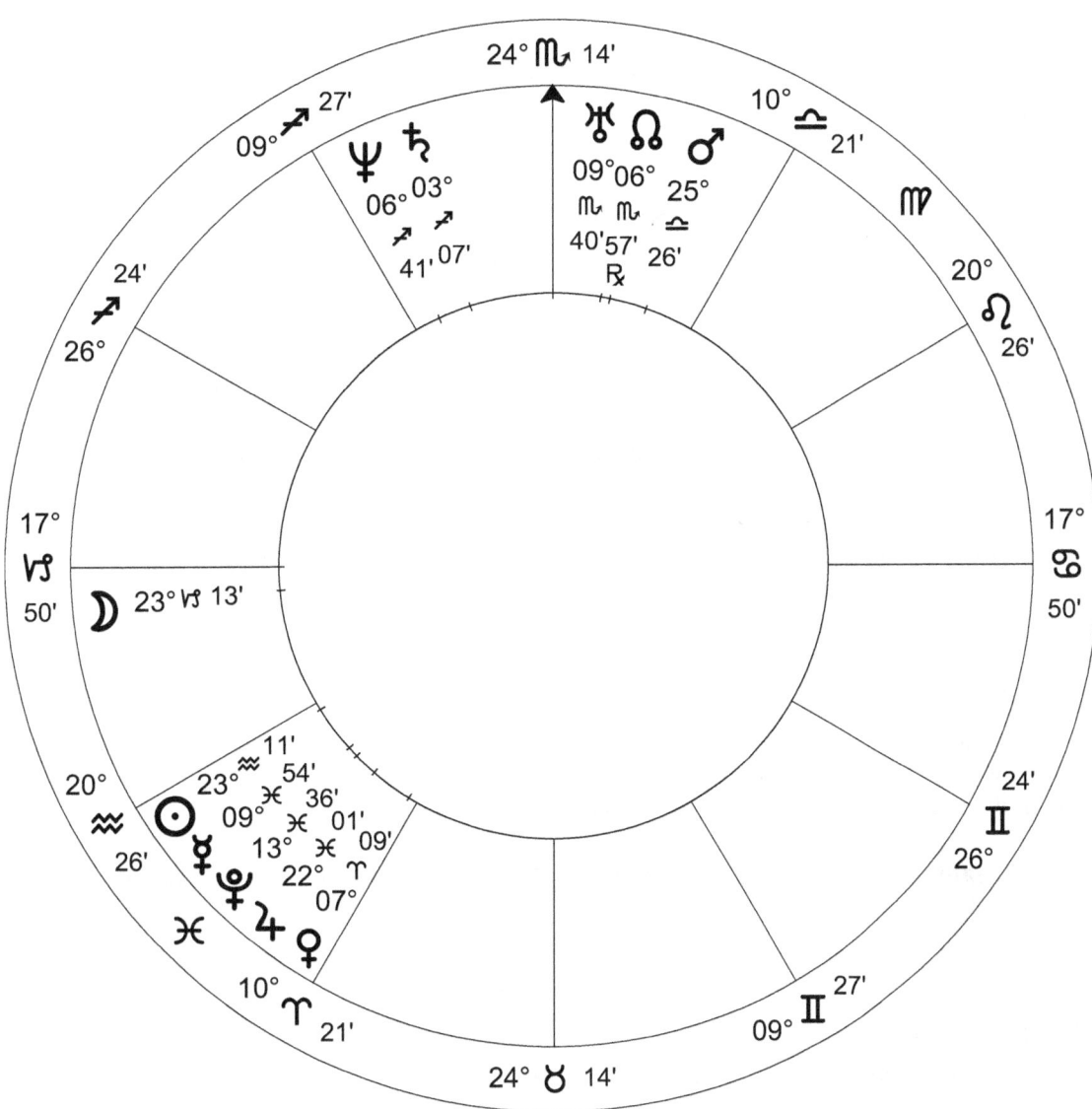

Charles Darwin, February 12, 1809, 6:00 am, Shrewsbury, England
Tropical, Koch

Transit and Solar Arc Pluto Aspects: Charles Darwin

Event	Date	Aspect Type
Pluto semisextile Pluto	June 6, 1834	Transit
Pluto semisextile Pluto	*January 9, 1839*	*Solar Arc*
Pluto semisquare Pluto	June 19, 1849	Transit
Pluto semisquare Pluto	*February 26, 1854*	*Solar Arc*
Pluto sextile Pluto	June 13, 1865	Transit
Pluto sextile Pluto	*June 4, 1869*	*Solar Arc*
Pluto square Pluto	August 17, 1896	Transit
Pluto square Pluto	*May 5, 1900*	*Solar Arc*

Darwin's transiting and solar arc aspects pair up for a one-two punch about four or five years apart. Note that Pluto would have reached its square by transit at age 91. For Trump, Pluto will reach the opposition at about age 83! The difference reflects the immense difference in the pace of these two men's lives.

Other Planets

The rest of the planets fall in between the extremes of the Moon and Pluto cycles. Depending on retrograde periods, the progressed and transiting cycles will vary significantly, while the solar arc cycle, as usual, unfolds just as it does for all the planets. The differences in cycles suggest the less obvious mental and emotional nuances of each individual's life. The birth date for the following theoretical Mercury example was selected to illustrate this point.

Sample Mercury transit, Secondary Progressed, and Solar Arc Aspects

Event	Date	Aspect Type
Birth Date (12:01 a.m.)	March 27, 1945	
Mercury conjunction Mercury	April 9, 1945	Transit Retrograde
Mercury conjunction Mercury	May 12, 1945	Transit Direct
Mercury conjunction Mercury	May 21, 1957	Secondary Progression retrograde
Mercury conjunction Mercury	July 25, 1990	Secondary Progression, direct
Mercury semisquare Mercury	*May 6, 1991*	*Solar Arc*

Mercury sextile Mercury	*December 10, 2006*	*Solar Arc*
Mercury semisextile Mercury	November 11, 2010	Secondary Progressed
Mercury semisquare Mercury	April 27, 2018	Secondary Progressed
Mercury sextile Mercury	March 16, 2025	Secondary Progressed
Mercury square Mercury	*November 7, 2038*	*Solar Arc*
Mercury square Mercury	March 30, 2040	Secondary Progressed

Notice that by about ten days after the birth date, Mercury had turned retrograde and formed a conjunction to the natal Mercury on April 9. Mercury then turned direct and formed another conjunction on May 12. This means that the forward motion of Mercury was delayed or inhibited for almost six weeks in this hypothetical person's life.

Looking down the sample table, we see that Mercury by secondary progression forms a retrograde conjunction at age twelve, and a direct conjunction at age forty five. The period of thirty-three years between the conjunctions marks a substantial portion of the lifetime when this planet's energy is acting somewhat differently than expected.

On a personal note, I physically and emotionally felt the two-week time span when my Mercury turned direct by secondary progression. I was agitated, and I wanted to get moving! There was a major shift in my outlook and in the way I addressed the world. I had previously told other people that I felt like I was backing into new experiences; trying to reclaim something I had already learned. After Mercury turned direct, I felt that I was facing life more directly.

I can only imagine how our hypothetical person would experience the progressed Mercury conjunction to natal Mercury at ages twelve and forty-five, first retrograde and then direct. Remember, this progressed aspect will never happen for most people. Also remember, the progressed conjunctions are a reflection—a replay—of the transiting Mercury conjunction, then retrograde, and then direct again. Whatever occurred in those first weeks of life will be replayed, consciously or unconsciously, by progression at a later date.

Retrograde Periods

How should we interpret retrogrades? If you read five books, you will very likely get five different answers. First let us consider the "reality" of retrogrades. Then we will look at the ways they manifest in natal, progressed, and transiting charts vis-à-vis development.

Of course, the physical reality is that there are no retrogrades. After all, if planets really retrograded, they would fall out of orbit. The reality is that the planets are always direct in motion, and that they all go around the Sun in the same direction. They also all have relatively regular speed, although the more elliptical the orbit, the more the speed can vary from day to day. There is a lot more that can be said about retrograde motion.

What You See Is What You Get

From our geocentric perspective, all of the planets appear to retrograde. The frequency of retrograde periods and the length of each period varies according to the planets' orbits. Mercury retrogrades three or four times a year, for example. Venus and Mars retrograde periods occur once in about a two-year period. The rest of the planets retrograde once a year. Each year Mercury is retrograde about 60 to 72 days, Venus about 40 to 43 days, Mars 58 to 80 days, Jupiter 120 days, Saturn 140 days, Uranus 155 days, Neptune 157 days, and Pluto 160 days. Venus and Mars will not retrograde during some years at all. With all these variables, timing and interpretation of retrogrades where development is concerned turns out to be a theme well worth considering.

Retrogrades and Human Development

Retrogrades close to the birth date represent a map of possible developmental hiccups or delays. While we might think, based on earlier literature, that a retrograde necessarily represents a developmental problem, this is not always the case. Retrogrades at or close to the time of birth can have lifelong implications, as seen through the secondary progressions. The delineation of retrogrades is complex and requires consideration of the planet, the timing, and the progressed implications, if any.

Retrogrades in the Birth Chart

Retrogrades in the birth chart are widely believed to indicate some debilitation of a planet's influence. However, there is no universal agreement on this point. Llewellyn George stated: "The planet's influence does not change when retrograde, but the individual's response to the particular influence of that planet is different; the channel for expression of its special qualities or characteristics is not quite as good when retrograde as when direct in motion."[2]

Noel Tyl states: "Retrogradation in astrology is a very pertinent measure of inferiority feelings—in the sense of stimulus to self-improvement—especially Saturn retrograde. We know that retrogradation is a counterpoint within the scope of meaning of the particular planet." Each retrograde planet indicates an area of the life where effort must be made to lift the person to a higher level of that planet's expression. Tyl, pursuing Adler's theory of inferiority, suggests that retrograde planets show us where an individual gains tremendous strength by searching within himself or herself for answers.[3]

Kevin Burk presents a strong argument that any retrograde in the birth chart indicates an area where the individual is working on evolutionary issues during this lifetime. He describes the difference between growth and evolution this way: Growth is a rather regular cycle, year to year, within one lifetime, whereas evolution "encompasses soul lessons that usually require more than one lifetime to integrate and complete." He then goes on to say: "Planets in direct motion are operating on the growth level. Planets in retrograde motion are operating on the evolutionary level."[4] Therefore, retrograde Mercury is not just a different style of communication, or a weaker expression of the planet's energies. Mercury's expression occurs at the soul level. The equipment (Mercury) is the same, but the task (evolution) is very different. The same effect is true for all the planets, according to their nature.

Progressed Retrograde Cycles

Most people will experience a Mercury change of direction by progression at some point in their lives. Depending on when the rest of the planets retrograde, many of us have the outer planets retrograde for the entire lifetime. Venus and Mars retrogrades by progression are less common because of the short periods they are retrograde and the reduced frequency of their retrograde periods. In this chapter and throughout the book, you will find examples of planets changing direction soon after birth. We generally have very little information about anyone's infancy. However, in a study of twins that I undertook a number of years ago, I identified crises associated with planets that were stationary at birth. When medical crises occurred and one twin died, the reasons for the death were obviously associated with the planet (s) that were stationary.[5] This study cemented the idea in my mind that stations and retrograde periods were significant.

Research for this book convinced me that retrogrades on the birth date or soon thereafter have a potential effect on the early physical development. My working theory was that a retrograde planet could indicate a delay in a particular developmental process because the planet was delayed in reaching specific aspects to its birth position that coincide with developmental processes. This turned out to be true to a degree, but not completely. For example, an individual might not experience the first semisextile of Mercury or Venus for many months, and yet proceed completely normally along developmental paths associated with these planets. However, personality traits may be set in place during the retrograde periods that affect future interests or relationships.

A more significant finding, I believe, is that an early retrograde provides a period of time for consolidation of development. This is especially true of the personal planets that are so central to physical, mental, and social development in infancy and early childhood. For example, if Mercury retrogrades before it reaches the first square , the child has some time to consolidate mental and speech development. Parents sometimes note periods when a child seems to forget something that seemed to be well learned, and then remember it a few weeks later. These periods often coincide with transiting Mercury retrograde periods.

Because we seldom have detailed records of infant development, we find most of our examples by examining progressed retrogrades in client charts. For example, a woman decided to move to a different state and take a job uniquely suited to her talents in the year when Neptune turned retrograde by progression. In addition, during the coming years she continued a study of contemplative practice and took refuge in the Buddha.

Two Men Born the Same Day

If they should live long enough, these men will experience seven progressed planetary stations during their lives:

Comparison of Progressed Stations for Two Males Born the Same Day

Approximate Age	Station	Male 1 Date	Male 2 Date
Age 15	Venus Retrograde	June 3, 1962	October 30, 1962
Age 29	Mercury Retrograde	May 31, 1976	October 28, 1976
Age 33	Pluto Retrograde	December 31, 1979	May 27, 1980
Age 39	Saturn Retrograde	October 25, 1985	March 23, 1985
Age 49	Mercury Direct	April 30, 1996	September 26, 1996
Age 57	Venus Direct	August 14, 2003	January 11, 2004
Age 92	Neptune Retrograde	July 31, 2038	December 28, 2038

Note that these men were born 9 hours 50 minutes apart in actual time, in very different parts of the world. Most of this book deals with cycles that operate almost independent of actual birth time. However, due to birth time and place, the progressed planetary stations, reflect a substantial difference in the lives of these two men. The exact progressed stations occur almost exactly five months apart, with the earlier birth responding to later progressed stations.

The progressed dates produce a relatively large difference early in life, but in fact the developmental shift reflected in retrogrades is not usually dramatic. The shift is more a matter of a change of heart or a change in attitude toward the world over a period of time. Greater significance can be attached to the fact that each man experienced transiting aspects at nearly the same time, but they were associated with different progressed aspects.

Male 1

An interview with this man revealed the following: His life is clearly reflected by progressed stations. As a baby he had no appetite, we are told, and he was exceedingly thin and frail. His earliest memory is the fact that when he ran, his feet crossed each other. The later progressed retrogrades of Venus, Mercury, Saturn, Neptune, and Pluto provide a guide to many major events in his adult life, and some developmental markers in childhood. Mercury formed the opening

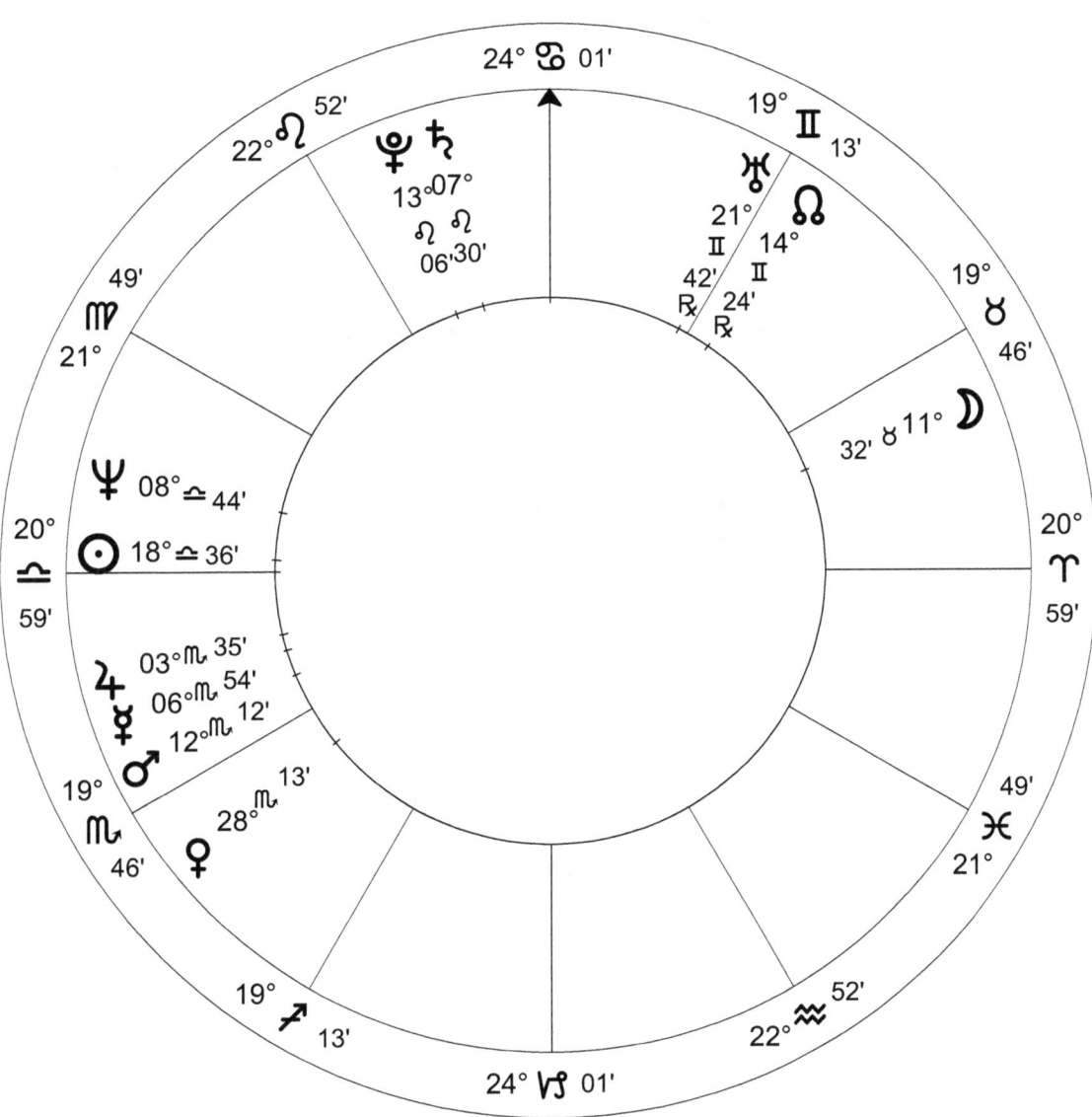

Male 1, October 12 1946, 6:20 am, Pueblo, Colorado
Tropical Koch

semisextile to the birth position by transit, and then immediately retrograded over that position. Venus refrained from the first semisextile within the first ninety days of his life by transit, and therefore within the first ninety years by secondary progression.

The only transiting retrogrades that dramatically affected the initial semisextile aspects were Mercury and Venus. Mercury reached the first semisextile about three days before it made the retrograde station. It then went from 7 Sagittarius back to 21 Scorpio, and then went direct to form the semisextile again on December 19. This delay in forward development comprised over half of his life at that early age. This was a dangerous period for him because he was not gaining mental and physical strength as anticipated.

Venus retrograded when he was fifteen days old, formed a conjunction with the birth position at age thirty one days, and turned direct at age fifty-seven days. He consolidated his social skills during this month. Siblings recall that he was a happy baby, except for the finicky eating.

At around the time progressed Venus turned retrograde, this man suffered a fractured sternum. This injury reflects the weakness in his bones that resulted in bowed legs. At this time he also managed the high school track team, demonstrating the capacity for social skills.

At about the time progressed Mercury retrograded, he went to work for the company from which he retired nearly thirty years later. A few months later he fell at work and broke his back, but made a good recovery. At the time progressed Mercury returned to direct motion, he could not identify any major events. However, his involvement in his church and in the lives of his children and grandchildren expanded over a period of years surrounding this event.

Transiting Pluto retrograded at age thirty-three days and returned to conjunct the birth position on December 18. Because of the duration of Pluto's retrograde period, it remains retrograde throughout his life. At age 33 when progressed Pluto retrograded, he earned the certification that insured his future career. Pluto retrograde reflects his lifelong odyssey in search of religious and spiritual meaning. Although he never became a priest or minister, he did seriously consider that profession around the time of his progressed Venus retrograde, and his life has been filled with active ministry to family, friends, and associates.

I have left Saturn for last. This man's transiting Saturn turned retrograde thirty-nine days after he was born, and returned to the natal position forty days later. This means that Saturn by progression will conjunct natal Saturn when he is seventy nine years old. About six months before the progressed Saturn retrograde station, he and his family chose to make church a regular part of their lives. A few months after the station, he suffered a serous eye injury that led to lens replacement and a cornea transplant.

From a spiritual perspective, Saturn reflects the responsible approach this man has taken to his life. He is a loyal brother, a faithful husband, and is active in the lives of his children and grandchildren. His religious convictions have guided his life. Not a formal person, he is very diplomatic, and capable of carrying on a conversation about just about any subject with just about anyone.

Male 2

Not every person will have dramatic events that mark the progressed stations of the planets. Our second example demonstrates the more internal expression of the stations.

This man has no detailed record of events in his infancy. He stated he had his tonsils removed at about age fifteen, roughly coincident with the Venus retrograde station by progression. No other illnesses or developmental issues were noted. He stated his feeling that he spent the years when Venus was retrograde seeking to make other people happy. He never married.

At the time of the Mercury retrograde station around age thirty, he said that he was doing a lot of writing, teaching, and consulting work. He noted that his focus turned toward concentration, more serious thinking, and an intense, practical attitude toward life. His writing began to slow down. Most of his books were written before this time.

No events or shifts in attitude were noted around the time of the Pluto retrograde station.

By the time of the Saturn retrograde station at age forty, his writing had shifted almost exclusively to revision of existing work, with no major writing after this time. Similarly, no major events were linked to the Mercury direct station, except that he became more active in a professional organization.

The Venus direct station by progression when he was fifty-four marked the beginning of a period when he began to focus more on making himself happy. Relationships have not developed into anything permanent, and he did lose interest in a relationship that began while Venus was still retrograde by progression.

The lives of these two men have taken dramatically different directions, at least as seen by the progressed stationary positions of planets. Both have had productive careers, and both have interest in the spiritual or metaphysical side of life, although the specific focus is very different.

Often there will be no major events associated with the progressed stations. The degree of the station leaves a marker, however, that can be activated by transits later on. Conditions or events associated with these transits to the stationary degree often have a fantasy or thoughtful quality rather than physical events occurring at a specific time.

18/The Astrology of Development

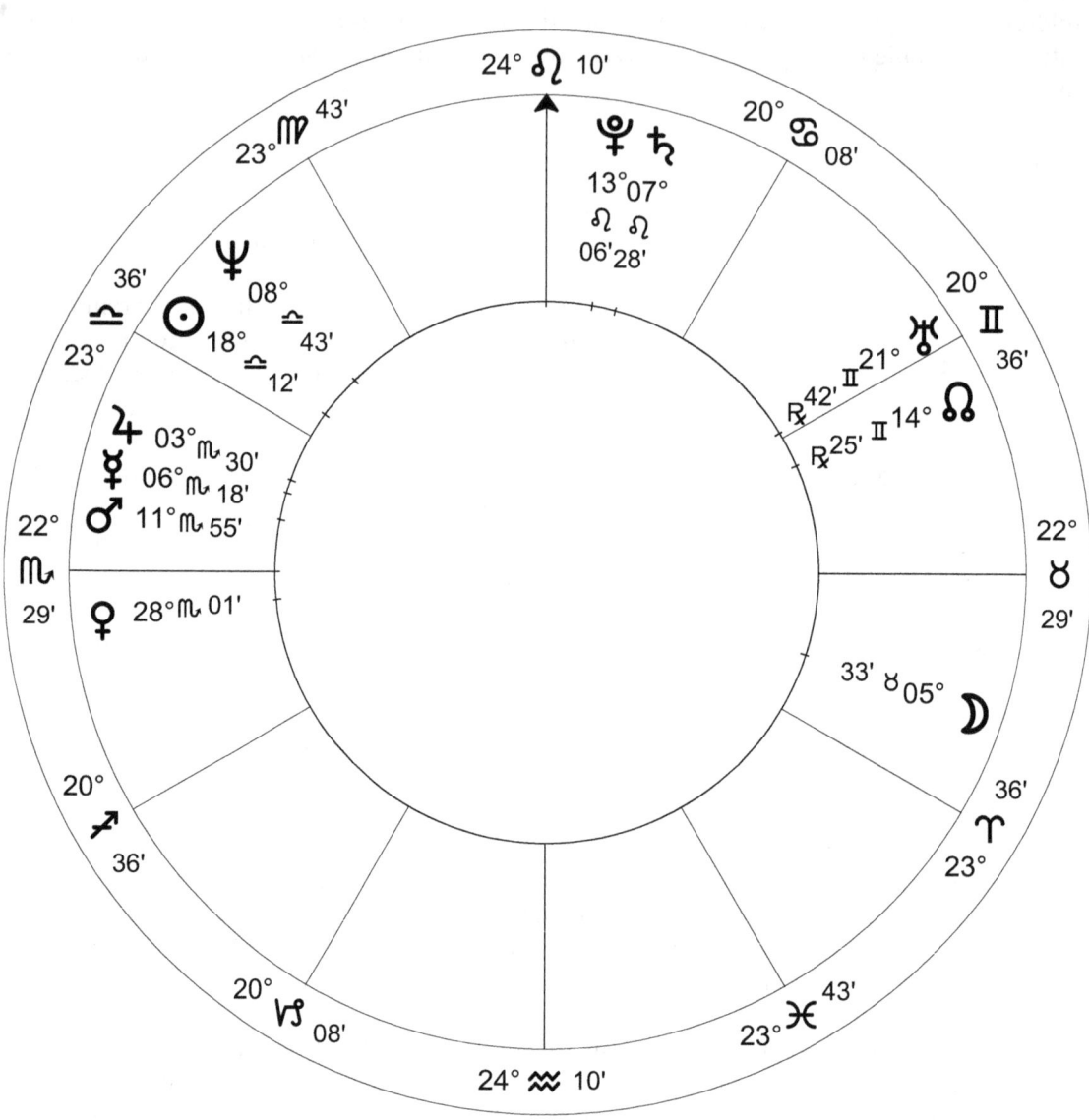

Male 2, October 12, 1946, 9:00 am, Pune, India
Tropical Koch

Summary

This chapter has introduced some of the complexities of planetary cycles. The rest of the book takes the planets in turn and considers how the cycles typically unfold. Data has been gathered from a variety of sources to delineate developmental steps and the ages when they naturally occur. Thus we can identify what "ought" to happen at a certain time if life follows the "normal" path. We can also gather from the client any information about what actually happened at specific times. By combining the two sets of information, we get a clearer picture of the individual's developmental processes.

Finally, I wish to note that human development doesn't magically stop on the twenty first birthday or at the first Saturn return. Development continues throughout our lives, and a case can even be made that development continues after we pass into another state of existence after death. Certainly this seems true for people whose legacy continues after they are gone.

Chapter Three

The Moon

The timing of the first lunar aspects to the birth chart is quite regular, with a potential variation of only a half day or so. The first days of an infant's life, assuming there was near-term pregnancy, also follow a very predictable pattern. In order to thrive, the baby must eat, sleep, and be protected from the cold. It needs to be touched and emotionally nourished as well. After all, up until birth it was in the constant company of the mother. After birth, the baby needs, if not constant contact, a great deal of attention.

For premature babies, each crisis is more dramatic. The hurdles to growth are greater, and underdeveloped organs are severely challenged. In fact, premature birth is the major issue for peri-natal survival. In such cases the timing of events may be quite different for months or even years, as the baby has to "catch up" to expectations. Therefore, applying many of the guidelines in this book to premature infants has to take the physical realities of shorter term pregnancy into consideration.

Throughout this book I present guidelines for timing child development, and I hope you think of them as guidelines only, and not rigid evaluations. They are not a measuring stick against which to evaluate a child, nor expectations that each child should meet. They do outline the developmental processes that occur, and the typical or so-called "normal" order if these processes. All children, premature or not, vary from the standard in some respects.

While it is less true for the Moon than for the Sun and planets, there are some variations in the lunar cycle. However, they never amount to a full day's difference during the first month of life. The Moon's speed allows us to explore precise timing of events each day. When considering the secondary progressed Moon, variations in speed result in substantial differences in timing. During some years the progressed Moon will move nearly fifteen degrees, while during other years the motion will be closer to eleven degrees, therefore affecting the precise timing of major events in one's life.

Neo-Natal Developmental Tasks

Once past the first few minutes after birth, when a baby must take its first breath, there are still monumental challenges to healthy development. The Moon's first passage through the birth chart provides a refined view of what the personal challenges are. The following section considers the major developmental tasks associated with the Moon in astrology, based on the aspects of the Moon to its place in the birth chart.

Information for each aspect, age, and developmental process or issue is as follows:

Conjunction—Birth

Babies are born with a remarkable set of capabilities. This book is not the place to list every detail, but I do want to state that the miracle of life is captured astrologically in the meanings of the Sun, giver of life, and the Moon, builder of form. Babies have a full set of physical functions and are more resilient than I ever imagined before my own children were born. Some basic reflexes associated with the Moon are as follows:

- Rooting reflex—nourishment. This reflex is activiated when babies seek the nipple and begin to suckle.
- Babiski reflex—toes flair when foot is gently stroked. This reflex indicates a normal neurological function, and is a measure of the maturity of the nervous system.
- Movement of arms and legs on both sides of the body equally well.
- Palmar grasping reflex. This reflex actually disappears, but is a significant indicator of neurological and physical development. Newborns have remarkable strength in their hands.

The Moon is often portrayed in astrology as an indicator of nourishing and nurturing qualities. In the first month of an infant's life, nourishment is the key to growth and development, so it should be no surprise that the Moon is the central figure in transits during that time.

Square—6.8 Days

As the baby nurses and develops some skill at this vital function, weight gain naturally occurs. Babies have begun to gain weight by this first point of balance, and they are on the road to successful growth and development. There are many challenges ahead, but the first hurdle of independent life has been overcome.

Example: I had the opportunity to be closely involved with the birth of a friend's baby and his first few weeks of life. This child was full term, although rather small. There were some difficulties in nursing. He didn't seem able to take the nipple and nurse properly. Supplemental feedings were easier because the flow from a bottle is easier. The baby was rather fussy, and the mother became exhausted. The mother then consulted La Leche League for help with nursing. After a very short time, the baby gained the necessary skill and strength to nurse properly, and the crisis was overcome.

Here we see the importance of appropriate medical care for infants. The mother didn't really know how nursing should work, and just a little bit of extra help solved what could have been a life-threatening problem. The point of understanding the developmental cycles throughout this book is this:

- We can understand the challenges we face at any age.
- We can perceive individual differences.
- We can seek appropriate help at any stage.
- We can understand challenges better if we know what we are facing.

In each chapter you will find indications of the developmental tasks of each planet, along with suggestions for how to apply the information when working with yourself and others.

Opposition—13.7 Days

The baby settles into a routine. By this time there may be more regular hunger patterns, although a pattern may not emerge this early. The parents will have become more familiar with the baby's needs, and will exert their influence to establish an orderly cycle to some extent.

The baby will likely demonstrate different responses to daylight and darkness. Parents hope the baby will adapt quickly to a typical schedule of being awake more during the day and asleep more at night, and signs of awareness of daylight are often observed as early as age two weeks.

Parents may observe a lack of "cooperation" on the part of the baby. Please remember that infancy is not about the baby cooperating! It's about the care givers learning how to care for the infant.

As early as two weeks, the baby may recognize the mother. Some child development books suggest that a newborn cannot see the mother clearly, so there is a lot of disagreement about this. However, infants may already recognize the "feel" of each person who holds them.

At this point there is a developing awareness of being in the world. The baby may respond to voices or other sounds in some way; it may not be an organized response, but more of a reflexive movement.

After only a few days of adjusting to life in the world, the baby may eat more regularly, sleep more regularly, and have regular periods of being awake that are unrelated to physical demands of diapers and food. However, don't be surprised if regularity is not part of the picture for several more weeks. Parents should not be overly concerned if a two-week-old infant does not respond in all these areas.

Square—20.5 Days

The typical baby is gaining size and strength. Movements of limbs are more organized, and the baby may lift its head. Some vocalization occurs, aside from crying.

The baby pays attention to people and things within the visual range, which may be rather small. Recognition of immediate household members is likely, and some vocal response to talking may occur. Facial expressions become clearer. The baby may smile in response to a voice or a smile. Physical movements are stronger. By this time the baby has developed some personality. In fact, babies are born with personalities, as most parents will attest. However, by three weeks there has been some adjustment of baby to parents and parents to baby, and the baby's unique personality begins to revel itself clearly.

Conjunction—27.3 Days

The infant can probably turn its head sideways (reminiscent of the newborn rooting reflex). Infants also move limbs using large, jerky movement. They normally move arms more than legs; turn the head from side to side; raise the chin, lie with the head turned to one side; support the head a little when pulled up slightly; make reflexive forward walking movements when held in the air; and demonstrate that the palmar grasping reflex still present.[6]

Clearly, by one month, when the Moon has returned to its own place for the first time, an infant has made major progress in strength, movement, and social arenas, as well as eating and digesting nutrients. The attentive parent or caretaker has observed progress each day, perhaps without registering any dramatic changes.

Progressed Moon Cycle

In the same way that the first lunar cycle is representative of the events in the lives of all newborns, the progressed Moon delineates patterns throughout life. Because the Moon is always direct in motion, this cycle is more regular than the cycles of planets. Thus the progressed lunar cycle can be compared to a musical metronome—it marks out the timing of life in a regular way for everyone. The errant retrograde periods of the planets can be viewed as the moments in a piece of music when the tempo changes. If the tempo of a transit speeds up ahead of the metronome, then we see early development, whereas retrograde planets at the time of an expected lunar progressed aspect may indicate delays in development. Over the long haul, the cycle of Saturn's transit may closely parallel the progressed Moon, as the cycles are close to the same length. The cycles of the other planets fit into these two, and show the "color" of individual developmental processes.

The following list indicates developmental processes we can expect at certain stages of the first complete progressed lunar cycle.

Information about the progressed lunar cycle, aspect, age, and developmental process or iIssue is as follows:[7]

Semisextile—2.25 Years

Intense "work" takes place on the part of the child to grow and learn. Although attention spans are often rather short, the intensity of effort can be seen on the child's face, and felt in the tensing of other muscles.

Sextile—4.5 Years

The child uses every opportunity to imitate the parents and others in the immediate environment. Social learning accelerates. Children are more willing to carry on a conversation, talk on the telephone, and express their ideas to parents and others.

Square—6.8 Years

This age marks the first attempt to disengage emotionally from the mother. The child enters formal schooling. This period can be challenging, as the child will switch from being receptive to being proactive, both at home and at school. The switching back and forth will be inconsistent, and abrupt. Sometimes the child's actions will be very independent, and at other times he or she will fall back into old patterns.

At this age children understand the concept of opposites, like hot and cold. They can talk about the opposite of something. They can explain differences between two objects. They can trace a path through a simple paper and pencil maze. They grasp the concepts associated with words like because, under, already, and not yet. They can pronounce and distinguish all vowel sounds.

Another big intellectual step usually seen by this age is the capacity to grasp the basics of logic. While they probably understood consequences well before this time, now children can formulate possibilities in a more logical way. The ability to draw conclusions is necessary for the capacity to foresee the results of one's actions, and plays a big part in the understanding of right and wrong, a quality attributed to the first square of Saturn to its birth place at around this age (see Chapter Eight).

Trine—9.1 Years

The child begins to define abstract words and can give reasons for rules. He or she has different styles of conversation for different people. Can give "hints." Feels capable about life.

Quincunx—11.37 Years

The child can memorize without any reflection upon meaning, but may have a hard time paraphrasing something.

Opposition—13.7 Years

The teen has greater emotional awareness (of self and perhaps of others). This is a period where greater objectivity may emerge as well. The Moon reflects instinctual responses, and the opposition by progression signals a period during which we are more aware of those responses coming from within us. We may also be more curious about how these responses work for other people.

Quincunx—15.92 Years

By this time maturation of thought processes has probably occurred. After gaining awareness of instinctual responses, teens gain the capacity for abstract thinking. This lunar progression often coincides with the first Saturn opposition, and this pairing of the Moon and Saturn reflects the two capacities required for abstract thinking: an inner sense of the unseen, and an outer awareness and capacity for analysis in the concrete world.

Trine—18.2 Years

Teens have generally graduated from high school and have settled into a job or college life. This is a comfortable period for many teens, during which they feel fewer emotional pressures. There may be a bit freer approach to life in general.

Square—20.5 Years

This aspect is similar to the opening Saturn square, but on the emotional side. While Saturn has more to do with the structure of the outer life, the Moon relates to the inner developmental process.

Sextile—22.75 Years

Future opportunities are taken more seriously, perhaps because more opportunities present themselves. There are chances for the individual to explore emotional desires and make decisions about the future.

Semisextile—25 Years

This period could bring emotional doubts that accompany potential opportunities.

Conjunction—27.3 Years

This aspect often occurs near the time of the Saturn return by transit, but reflects more of an emotional developmental tone. There is a sense that emotional facets of the personality are coming together into a unit, and that the individual can apply emotional criteria to decision-making processes, as well as logical and practical considerations. This period often signals the end of childhood from the emotional perspective.

The metaphor of the first lunar passage through the birth chart can be extended to each planet's first passage as well. By an overwhelming margin, the most significant lunar task in the first month relates to nutrition, at least on a level most of us can perceive. For each of the other planets, there is also a primary developmental task or set of tasks, and we will examine them in terms of the planetary cycles and in developmental terms.

The first lunar challenge, and the comparable challenge for each of the visible planets, will be reprised in a different way just after the Saturn return, which occurs around age twenty-eight to thirty. At that time the adult enters the second phase of life - a phase where productivity becomes a primary goal. In the days and weeks following the Saturn Return, the individual experiences a rebirth of sorts, and we can look at the first cycle of the Moon and inner planets following the Saturn Return to gather information about how the productive period between the approximate ages of thirty and sixty will proceed.

For people whose Saturn transits its natal place only once around age 28 or 30 (no retrograde pattern), there is a direct, straightforward path to follow. For individuals who experience three transits of Saturn to its natal place in short succession (retrograde pattern), the path is not so sure, or the entrance on the path is punctuated by a reversal and re-starting process.

A third developmental cycle begins at the second Saturn Return, and another set of initial transits of the planets punctuates one's movement into the latter phase of life.

The Lunar Phase

The lunar phase (the angle between the Sun and Moon) in the birth chart is often used to describe the emotional or psychological approach to life. Other authors have interpreted lunar phases in great detail. I will only touch on key factors for each repetition of the phase angle. The Sun-Moon phase angle is repeated every month and provides a strong reminder of the specific mental / emotional bent of the individual. As such, there is a time each month when an individual can readily refocus and adjust his or her direction to suit the natural inclination. In terms of development, this phase cycle marks a regular "check in" system. If we are looking for the signals, we can get a clear sense of how this check-in mechanism works in ourselves and in our children.

The Sun-Moon phase angle occurs monthly in each of the succeeding signs. While you will want to consider the Sun and Moon signs in your evaluation of the phase angle, the discussion here is limited to the phase angle itself and highlights the nature of the phases. Most of us will not be born exactly on the phases listed here. Measure the angle from the Sun to the Moon in the birth chart, and use the phase that occurred before that degree. For example, my Moon is 24 degrees from the Sun, so I will look at the conjunction.

- New (conjunction)—The individual expresses through instinctual responses. These are subjective responses that can be surprising to the individual and to other people. In terms of developmental processes, we can expect the individual to regroup on a less conscious level and then come out with a new expression or direction, based on the unconscious process.
- Crescent (semisquare)—This phase indicates a person who is consciously striving to separate from past limitations and move forward. Developmentally, this could signal the time each month when the individual strives hardest to learn a new task and make strong gains.
- First Quarter (square)—Challenges, mostly coming from the surrounding environment, drive decisions and action. However, the individual will also challenge the ideas of others, especially after the person has gained life experience and learns that life is a two-way street. This individual knows how to make choices.
- Gibbous (sesquisquare)—A search, albeit somewhat unconscious, for ways and means to accomplish whatever needs to be done. Insights and effort go hand in hand. This person often tests an idea or a plan internally, running through the entire process mentally in order to gauge the end result before starting into action.
- Full (opposition)—This phase indicates full awareness of the purpose of one's actions,

and there is more consciousness and objectivity than in previous phases. The world and its intricate patterns are revealed. However, this individual may be less able to relate to the concept of new beginnings, and also may feel separated from the phenomenal world.
- Disseminating (sesquisquare)—This phase represents the capacity to teach and to share. This phase brings inner agitation because the individual feels like he or she is too far ahead of the game to interact effectively with others. Within this phase there develops a satisfaction in the form of increased tolerance for self and others.
- Last Quarter (square)—This may be the point of maximum active power because the individual has gained experience and learned how to use his or her talents and skills. Effective action can occur more readily now, as the individual is fully and consciously informed from within and from the environment.
- Balsamic (semisquare)—This phase signals a heightening of intuitive capacity. The individual can foretell coming events and make plans to let go of thinking that is no longer useful. There is a bit of the prophet at work here, although other people may be skeptical about some of the fresh ideas that are forming.
- Dark of the Moon (just before next conjunction)—I find there is a significant difference between the Moon applying to a conjunction with the Sun and the Moon separating from the conjunction . The applying Moon has a profound anticipatory quality, whereas the separating Moon seems to have a more active, direct, although less conscious expression.

To summarize, each person experiences multiple Sun-Moon relationships:

- The relationship in the natal chart.
- The movement of the Moon through the natal chart, forming each phase angle.
- The repetition of the natal phase angles of the Moon to planets, marking a check-in time each month.
- The transiting Moon and its phases.
- The secondary progressed Moon's movement through the natal chart.

While some astrologers continue to consider more and more factors, the richness of the Sun-Moon relationship can provide a detailed map of individual development throughout life.

Fertility

Without getting into exhaustive examples of how the lunar phase cycles unfold, here is one telling factor: In general, women tend to become pregnant far more easily when the Sun / Moon lunar phase is the same as in the birth chart. This means that if their actual menstrual rhythm is out of synch with the astrological rhythm, there may be difficulties, or they may become pregnant at unexpected times of the month. If the menstrual cycle is longer or shorter than the lunar phase cycle, pregnancy may have to wait until the two cycles are aligned in order to have fertility peaks in both cycles.

The following chart provides an example of how this process works. I have included a column of dates when the lunar phase is the same as in the birth chart, and a column showing how the optimum date in the menstrual cycle lines up wit the lunar phase. In this example the woman has a thirty-four day menstrual cycle, and the predicted best date to conceive is on the twentieth day of the cycle.

Example of Menstrual Cycle Compared to Natural Lunar Phase Fertility Cycle

Menstrual Cycle Begins	*Optimum Date*	*Date Lunar Phase Cycle Repeats*
April 10, 2000	April 30, 2000	April 29, 2000
May 14	May 24	May 29
June 17	July 7	June 27
July 21	August 10	July 26
	August 25	
August 24	September 13	September 23
September 27	October 17	October 22
October 31	November 20	November 21
December 4	December 24	December 20
January 7 2001	January 27, 2001	January 19, 2001

You can see that the alignment of the cycles starts off fairly close, and then diverges, coming back into alignment some months later. There is a skipped date on August 25 to account for the difference in the length of the cycles. Some sources claim that this method works in ninety eight percent of cases.[8] I know that it worked for a member of my family.

Reflected Cycles

An individual born December 14, 1942, has a Sun-Moon phase angle of 86°40' (the Moon-Sun angle is 273°20'). Due to premature birth, he weighed under five pounds. While otherwise healthy, he suffered from jaundice, not unusual in infants. Within two weeks he began to gain weight, and at the end of the first lunar cycle he was on his way to a healthy life. From early infancy, he demonstrated the capacity to resist being led by the adults in his environment. The only kind of guidance that worked was an appeal to reason, even in very early childhood.

The natal Sun is in the second house in Sagittarius, with natal Moon in the fourth in Pisces. In the crescent phase, there is a struggle to separate the limitations of the family (fourth house) and self worth (second house). The father, a Pisces, was a violent alcoholic who when drunk abused his children. It is no stretch to say that the father was not a nurturing influence. The mother, however, was a cooler voice of reason throughout his childhood, for the most part.

This man graduated from a well-respected school and had an excellent career in industry. He never married.

Within months of his first progressed lunar return, his mother becaame seriously ill and he faced the loss of a powerful nurturing influence in his life.

About two years later, the Sun-Moon relationship was again highlighted. Within months of the first progressed phase angle return, his father died. While this death did not reflect the loss of a nurturing parent, it did signal the end of dependence on parents for guidance and support.

Around the time of the second progressed lunar return in 1997, this man experienced a kitchen fire (note the continued focus on nurture) that nearly destroyed his home.

Very close to the date of the second progressed phase angle return, relatives of his own generation either moved into town or visited for extended periods of time, and his health improved. He is now retired, still living in his own home. He has an up-to-date kitchen where he can cook to his heart's content, and he is an excellent cook. He also gardens and cans produce each autumn.

Progressed Moon Example

The importance of the progressed Moon cannot be over-estimated. The Moon is involved in just about every major life event. The following example, while very dramatic, does illustrate the way the progressed Moon acts in the chart.

Twin boys were born in early 1949. They were very premature, and were not expected to survive. They were born five minutes apart, and during that time, the Ascendant changed so that in the earlier chart the Moon was above the horizon in the seventh house, while in the second chart, the Moon was below the horizon in the sixth. The second twin died very shortly after birth, around the time that his progressed Moon moved forward to oppose the Ascendant. (As a point of information, my research with twins consistently indicates that angular planets reflect strength in infant charts, compared to cadent planets.)

At the time the surviving twin's progressed Moon returned to conjunct the seventh house natal Moon, his wife was pregnant with his first child. At the second progressed Moon conjunction to the natal Moon, he was involved in several contracts for the design of assisted living housing.

32/The Astrology of Development

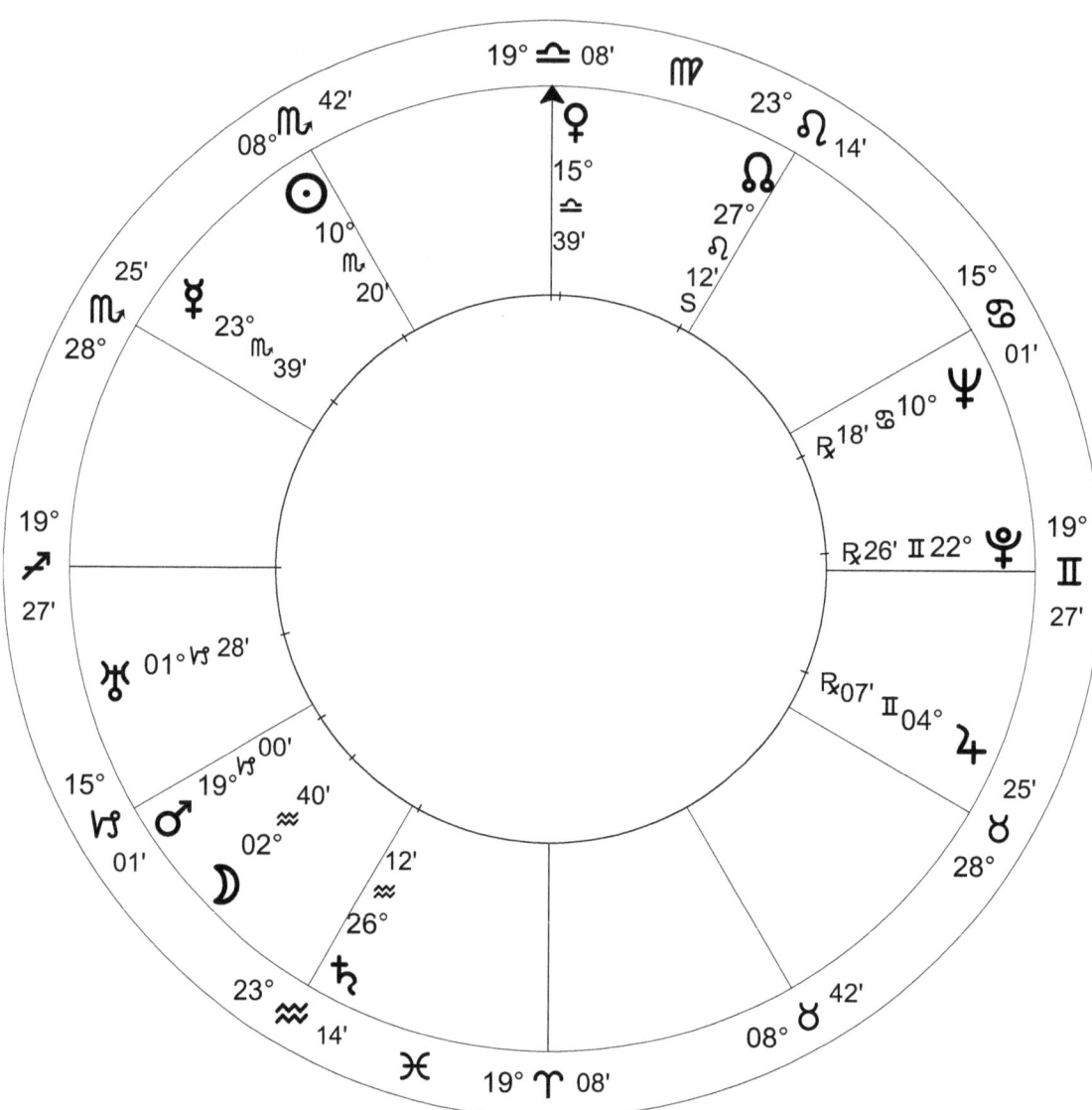

Arthur Young, November 3, 1905, 10:22:38 a.m., Paris, France
Tropical Koch

The three progressed Moon aspects reflect three different levels of nurturing in this man's life. The first progressed Moon aspect only occurred in the second twin's chart and reflected an insurmountable challenge. With natal Moon angular, this individual had the strength to assimilate nourishment and develop, even though significantly premature at birth. The progressed Moon conjunct the natal Moon reflects his capacity to enter into parenthood, while the second progressed Moon conjunction reflects the ability to nurture elders in our society.

Working with Phase Angles

If the angle is less than 180 degrees, it is in the opening, or less conscious phase. If the angle is more than 180 degrees, it is in the closing, or more conscious phase.

In Young's birth chart, the arc from the Moon to the Sun is 277°39'. This is a closing square (it is past 270 degrees). According to the lunar phases, this is the point of maximum active power and effective action, indicating success in public life. This certainly fits with his success in inventing and refining a helicopter design.

Let us consider the Moon-Sun phase for April 29, 1944 (see page 34), the day before Arthur Young's helicopter invention was announced by Bell Helicopter. The phase angle was repeated the day before his invention was announced. Certainly he knew on April 29 that his invention was a success, and this event confirms the power of his Moon-Sun phase angle.

Summary

With the Moon, and also with the Sun and planets, you can expect a constructive developmental process to be reflected in subsequent transiting phases, phase angle relationships, and progressed aspects. We will consider each of these as we look at the developmental processes associated with the Sun and each of the planets.

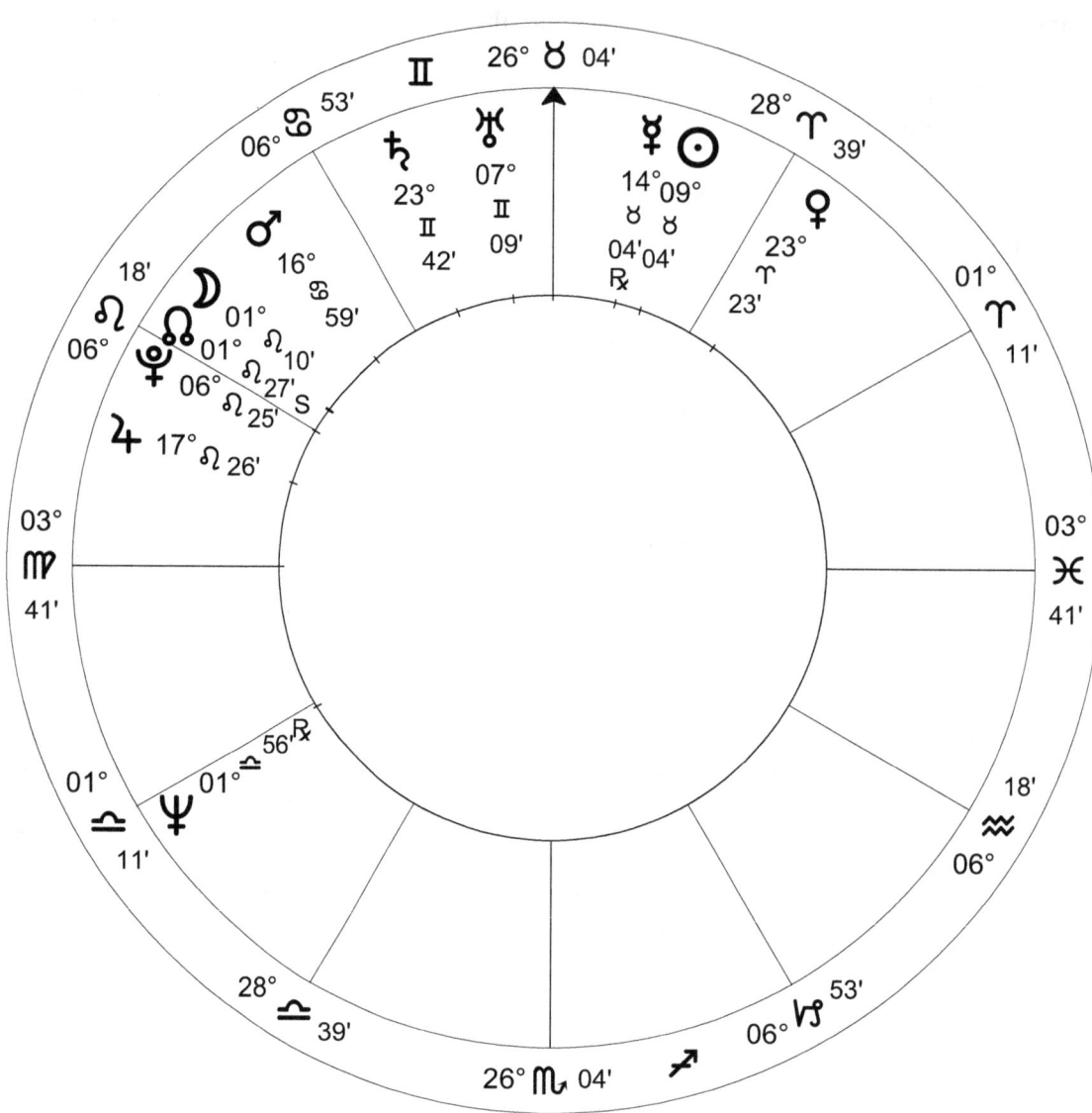

Arthur Young Phase Angle, April 29, 1944, 2:56:16 pm, Paris, France
Tropical Koch

Chapter Four

Sun, Mercury, and Venus Cycles

During the first year of life, intensive growth and development occur. Some of this is visible to the caretaker, but much of it is going on inside the body, specifically in the brain. During this first twelve months of life, a vast amount of growth and organization occurs that is essential to all future activities. This chapter takes a look at the cycles of the Sun, Mercury, and Venus to explore developmental patterns and to point out two important sets of information:

- The parallels of astrological cycles with human development.
- The evidence within astrological cycles of precocious or delayed development in infancy.

At this point I note that while normal development occurs in a specific, recognized, predictable way, factors in the environment play a huge role as well. For example, breast milk includes all the amino acids required for proper brain, muscle and other tissue development. Other foods may be deficient in these nutrients. Secondly, infants need larger amounts of iron and benefit from supplements in infancy. B vitamins are necessary for optimal tissue growth.

Another set of factors relate to the caretaker's desire and ability to provide security and love. Without other human contact, the baby's life lacks the enrichment of touch, conversation, and stimulation, all of which are needed for development, even at this very early age.

Because the focus for this book is on developmental cycles, environmental factors will be largely ignored. So too will transiting aspects and aspect patterns that indicate events and situations of all kinds.

The Sun, Mercury, and Venus cycles have been combined so that the interweaving of energies will become more evident. While retrograde periods are a basic fact of astrological life, their impact in terms of development can be seen clearly when the straightforward cycle of the Sun is contrasted to the possible variations in the cycles of the inner planets, particularly Venus. These variations show where advanced or delayed development can and do occur.

The following section takes each of the aspects of the Sun, Mercury and Venus to their respective birth positions and compares the timing of these aspects to observed developmental processes. Some of these will be familiar and others will be new to most readers. Research indicates that every observable stage of development, at least in the first year or two of life, is paralleled by specific growth, development, and organization within the brain. We will see that the ground is laid now for almost every human capacity.

The Sun—Sustainer of Life, Giver of Heat and Energy

The capacity to grow and thrive is demonstrated early. The Sun represents vitality—physical and mental vigor. This is the essential ingredient that distinguishes living things from non-living things. The Sun and its cycle indicate the natural progress of life, and the variations of the Sun's cycle are so small that whatever it reflects in terms of infant growth and development proceeds at the specified time. Once past the demands of the first month, as indicated in the chapter on the Moon, the Sun takes over as the central indicator of growth and progress. Central developmental issues during the first year relating to the Sun include:

- Oxygen in the blood.
- Heart and circulation.
- Cells and cell growth.
- Right side in males, left side in females.
- Acute fevers.
- Sense of individuality and separateness from others.

The regular forward motion of growth and development, as indicated by the Sun's motion, is accompanied by two patterns of greater or lesser regularity. I have included information about the more regular unfolding of Mercury and Venus patterns. Keep in mind that a retrograde Mercury period could signal a variation in time for the first transiting aspects to the natal position, or it could signal three passes. The Venus cycle incorporates an even larger potential discrepancy. For Venus I have included a range of days for each aspect. The sixty-eight day range for the opposition signals a developmental gap representing fully one third of the lifespan to date! That's a pretty big difference.

Let's consider that difference another way. At about age thirty, when the Sun makes its first semisextile by secondary progression, Venus could have done so as many as six years earlier, or Venus' semisextile could be as late as four years later. This difference reflects the vast range of potentially different social development for a young adult trying to make his or her way in the world. These years could seem like a lifetime!

Let's look at one more example. In the next chapter we note that Mars (physical development) can make its first opposition anywhere from age 343 days to 394 days, or about the same time the Sun makes its first conjunction. An early Venus conjunction at about nine and one-half months could signal social development that is well ahead of physical development. In contrast, a late Venus conjunction at about thirteen and one-half months puts physical development way ahead of social skills. The potential developmental difference between children, then, is four months. This reflects the difference between a child who babbles, says a few words, and generally socializes with family members and a child who rushes around engaging in every possible activity, while saying very little and demanding attention through crying and other behaviors. Those of you who are parents of two or more children probably relate very well to this kind of difference.

Mercury—Mind/Body Connection, Nervous System, Breath

Mercury-related development during the first year of life focuses on the brain and nervous system. Here are a few of the principal considerations:

- Brain function in general.
- The right cerebral hemisphere.
- Nerves involved with hearing.
- The larynx and speech.
- Nerves involved in voluntary muscle activity.
- Pulmonary circulation.
- An internal link between spirit and form.

Venus—Love, Capacity to Relate to Others, Organ Function

Venus developmental issues include physical growth and social development:

- Venous circulation.
- The process of cell reproduction.
- The Eustachian tubes in the ears.
- Kidneys.
- Thymus gland.
- Glandular products (hormones).

Most developmental challenges are far from life threatening. In addition, we can do a lot to prepare for what is coming through reading, studying the topic, and developing action plans. The following list shows the aspects of Sun, Mercury, and Venus to their natal position, and includes developmental processes or issues associated with the age, listed in days. There are also indications of how we can promote development. It is important to remember that "nurture" (the environment) is as big a factor as "nature" (what the baby is born with). Each baby has a timetable that is reflected in the astrology and aided or retarded by environmental factors. See the bibliography for sources of developmental information. For the sake of completeness, the list includes aspects for which no specific developmental marker has been identified in developmental psychology literature.

At birth: The brain has about 100 billion neurons.

Venus, 24/34 days, semisextile: Baby smiles, whether purposefully or accidentally. Infant prefers human faces over other shapes.

Mercury, 30 days, semisextile: The infant makes jerky arm movements, brings hands near the face, keeps the hands in tight fists, recognizes some sounds and voices, startles at loud noises, and quiets when spoken to. The infant may smile, and may increase or decrease sucking when spoken to. Parents may begin to notice different sounds the baby makes, other than crying.

Sun, 30 days, semisextile: Baby raises chest and turns head; head flops down toward back.

Venus, 49/68 days, sextile: Infant gazes at mother's face. This is the first sign of social competence. By four months, this tendency decreases.

Mercury, 60 days, sextile: Walking reflex may begin to disappear; grasping reflex also declines. This is a time when language capacity develops (using right hemisphere of brain)

Sun, 61 days, sextile: There is substantial eye movement.

Venus, 73/102 days, square: Baby may snuggle more comfortably when held.

Mercury, 90 days, square: Baby brings hands together, reaches for objects but usually misses. Can distinguish several hundred words. Repetition of words helps to establish neural pathways. Many rhythms in the baby's life become more regular. The infant opens and closes hands, and brings hands to mouth.

Sun, 91 days, square: Baby laughs out loud, pays attention to objects, follows objects past midline, smiles spontaneously. A shift in EEGs reflects a shift in sleep patterns.

Venus, 97/136 days, trine: Sensory integration occurs (i.e., appearance, taste, and smell associated with particular food). The baby is more easily consoled.

Mercury, 119 days, trine: Baby can look at and hold rattle at the same time; binocular vision and depth perception develop.

Venus, 122/170 days, quincunx; Sun, 122 days, trine: The back is much stronger; baby sits with support.

Venus, 145/204 days, opposition: Baby squeals, smiles, vocalizes and may say baby talk words, waves blow-kisses, learns mama and dada, and expresses joy. Baby is obviously more social by this time.

Mercury, 149 days, quincunx: Baby may start to grasp objects, and makes the connection between sound and gesture.

Sun, 152 Days, quincunx; Venus, 170/238 days, quincunx; Mercury, 179 days, opposition: The baby babbles, turns in direction of a voice, grasps or picks up small objects, says mama or dada indiscriminately, begins to learn concepts—"hear the cry," "soft bear!" There is an increase in range of sounds infant makes, and the baby notices that toys make sounds. The baby can hear the sounds of all languages and distinguish them. (This ability is lost at around age twelve months.) The crawling pattern and other voluntary locomotion develops. Curiosity is evident. What seems like babbling has become an apparent effort to reproduce specific sounds.

Sun, 183 days, opposition: Baby feeds himself or herself a cracker. He or she becomes somewhat demanding, and will object when a desire is not accommodated. Baby begins to socialize, wave, and laugh, learns names—mommy, daddy, own name. There is a sense of individuality and separateness.

Venus, 194/272 days, trine; Mercury, 209 days, quincunx: Baby can trade object from one hand to the other, and responds to his or her own name.

Sun, 213 days, quincunx: Baby turns over both ways.

Venus, 218/306 days, square: Baby plays ball or other simple games, fear of strangers may occur, and baby cries at nap time or bedtime. The connection is made between knowing something and feeling something about it. The baby become a "leg leech" and follows the caretaker everywhere.

Mercury, 239 days, trine: Cross pattern crawling develops.

Venus, 242/340 days, sextile: Baby demonstrates awareness of different colors.

Sun, 244 days, trine: Independent activity is evident.

Venus, 267/374 days, semisextile; Mercury, 269 days, square: The baby walks holding furniture, says mama, and may play patty-cake. He or she will use a method other than crying to communicate wants, and has the ability to hold the breath. Awareness of object permanence develops (the baby remembers things that are out of sight). A primitive capacity for hypothesis develops; for example, this can be seen in the irritating behavior of dropping toys to see if they always fall, and to see if someone will pick them up. The baby can crawl, cruise by holding onto furniture, and some are able to walk. The baby's "talk" seems to have rhythm and syntax, even though there may be no actual words.

Sun, 274 days, square: The baby looks for a dropped object, plays peek-a-boo, responds to simple directions, and shows emotional attachment to toys and other objects.

Venus, 291/408 days, conjunction: Alternately independent and clingy, the baby can mimic actions, scribble/draw, and enjoy picture books. The baby can read emotions in people's faces, tone of voice, and words. The baby may pause to consider reaction of the caregiver to his or her actions. Greater emotional control reflects frontal cortex development.

Mercury, 298 days, sextile: The baby practices language skills, even if the words don't make sense. Parents often perceive their own tones of voice and rhythms of speech in their babies, even though no actual words are spoken, or with the occasional "dada" included in a nonsense sentence.

Sun, 304 days, sextile; Mercury, 328 days, semisextile; Sun, 335 days, semisextile; Mercury, 358 days, conjunction: The baby may indicate wants without crying, say several words, or say a short sentence with baby talk words or actual words. The capacity to think through small problems reflects frontal cortex development. Memory and recall improve, as well as use of thumb and forefinger to grasp small objects. The baby can imitate words, shake head "no," and wave goodbye. He or she can use objects correctly (drinking cup, possibly hair brush), and can recognize pictures and look at the correct picture when it is named.

Sun, 365 days, conjunction: Separation anxiety may develop, and the child may have favorite clothes. Walking is a sign of independence.

Retrograde Periods

Another way to look at variations on the cycles of Mercury and Venus is retrogrades. The relative position of Earth to Mercury and Venus impacts the speedy forward movement of these planets. Two developmental issues may result:

- Developmental "forgetting" can occur when a planet retrogrades before it reaches a developmental marker (an aspect).
- In the long run, development may be enhanced by a retrograde because the child has extra opportunities to learn or develop in a certain way.

Similar developmental delays or enhancements will be seen with the outer planets. After infancy, a delay can signal the opportunity to watch other kids do something and learn from their behavior. Being first can be fun, but following the leader can be productive as well.

Considering the fact that all babies will experience three or more retrogrades of Mercury in the first year, it's easy to understand the developmental facts of language development in infants. Research has demonstrated that:

- Repetition of words and phrases helps the infant to learn them.
- Reading to infants and having conversations helps them to integrate language. Infants and small children love to hear the same story over and over again.
- When language is not part of the infant's environment, as was the case with large numbers of Romanian orphans during the latter part of the twentieth century, development of language was delayed or permanently impaired.

Caretakers benefit from knowing about the cyclical nature of development so they may be, for example, more willing to talk to the baby, even though the baby can't talk back. They may be more willing to read the same story, play the same music, or rerun the same video. They may be more responsive to whatever attempts the baby makes in the direction of language and communication.

Given the timing possibilities for a retrograde period of Mercury or Venus, as the retrograde relates to the normal expected dates for squares and oppositions to the birth position of each planet, what can we expect from variations from the norm, and more importantly, how can we use this information to insure healthy development in infants? First let's look at the potential variations from the expected three-six-nine-twelve month pattern for squares, oppositions, and conjunctions. Because the Sun, Mercury, and Venus follow each other closely, we can expect that all three will reach the first conjunction, or return, close to the same time, although the Venus cycle may have significant variation from this timing. This is not true for the intermediate square, opposition, and square.

Typically, the period from a Mercury direct station to the next retrograde station is about three months and eleven days. This means that a Mercury retrograde period can begin at any time from the day of birth forward to a little past the expected time for the first Mercury square. Mercury moves at a rate greater than a degree a day and moves about four and one-half signs between stations. This means that Mercury actually could make the square to its birth position in 2 months and one day. The following table provides an example of the potential difference in age at the first Mercury square.

Time Variance of First Transiting Mercury Square

Date	Mercury position	Station or Aspect	Days from Birth
March 25, 2006	13 Pisces 11	Direct Motion	0
May 26, 2006	13 Gemini 11	First square	62
July 4, 2006	1 Taurus 20	Retrograde Station	101
March 2, 2006	26 Pisces 55	Retrograde Motion	0
March 25, 2006	1 Gemini Pisces 11	Direct Station	23
June 2, 2006	26 Gemini	First square	92

We can see that the potential difference in time at the first Mercury square is very large—as much as one-third of the life. In addition, the example for the later square around the expected time incorporates a complete Mercury retrograde period into the first twenty-three days of life. What does this mean in terms of developmental expectations?

In the example above for a child born on March 25, 2006, we see that Mercury developmental processes race ahead at a much faster rate. This infant will very likely display sensitivity to noise and awareness that some noises, like conversation, are organized, while others are not. The baby may take short naps, be easily awakened, and will demonstrate a desire to be a part of everything that happens. He or she may show marked reluctance to go to sleep. By the same token, this baby will want to be awake when there is light, and may be more willing to sleep through most of the night, even at the age of one or two weeks.

The baby in the second example is a different story. Possibly more placid, this baby will nap for longer periods, will stay asleep through the normal noise of a household, and will be more laid back in every way. However, he or she may stay on the infant schedule for a few weeks longer, not sleeping through the night as quickly as the baby in the first example. This behavior indicates a more introverted style, one where information is taken in and considered. Learning may appear to occur in remarkable spurts, with motor and other skills mastered "in a moment," but actually only after significant internal processing.

Never fear, there is intense learning and development going on in both cases. The differences mark each baby's unique style and rhythm. Parents often know their child will be either a deep thinker or a mover-and-shaker before age one. My first child, born when Mercury was very fast, scooted across his entire bed within days of birth. My second child, born just after a Mercury station, slept very still in one spot and awakened more gradually. These differences continue to be reflected in adult life in significant ways.

Secondary Progression

The details of infant development are endless and fascinating to some readers. Astrologically, the implications of infant development are reflected in secondary progressions, providing a powerful model for a lifetime of development. It is easy to see that day for a year progression of the Sun, Mercury, and Venus will result in wide variations of timing throughout the life. At age thirty, there is already a potential six-year difference between Venus and the Sun. By age sixty this gap has widened to eleven years, and by age ninety to seventeen years. The smaller variations during the first year by transit have been magnified by day-for-a-year progressions. A Mercury retrograde period early in life will be experienced very differently from one that happens around age twenty or thirty. Many people will not experience Mercury or Venus retrograde by progression in their lifetimes.

Differences in the timing of infantile social development, such as gaining the capacity to smile or gaze at the mother's face, translate into lifelong differences in the capacity to relate to another individual. For example, the early development of a smile will encourage the parents to play and to give more attention. This in turn builds not only social competence, but social confidence. At age twenty-four to thirty, around the time of the comparable progressed aspects, these two qualities—social competence and confidence—are critical to the development of strong friendships and romantic ties. Thus the speed of Venus transits early in life present a model for one's later social capacity. Venus retrograde may also indicate specialized development of harmony and balance that most of us will never experience.

Oprah Winfrey

Oprah Winfrey has become one of the wealthiest people on the planet, and certainly a very successful individual. She has first-rate communication skills. About a month after she was born, Mercury turned retrograde. It turned direct again without forming a conjunction with her birth Mercury. This suggests that her verbal abilities developed in a straightforward way in early infancy.

In contrast, a person born around February 13, 1954, would have experienced Mercury retrograde conjunction natal Mercury at age two weeks, and another conjunction when Mercury was direct at about age six weeks. For an infant, this might have signaled a period during which there was an interruption of progress, such as might be caused by an ear infection or other illness. Or it might have coincided with one of the rather common periods during which little outward evidence of communication occurs; but a lot of brain development is taking place.

In looking at secondary progressions for Oprah, her progressed Mercury turned retrograde December 16, 1975, and turned direct April 7, 1998. Some of Oprah's greatest accomplishments took place during this period, so we know that Mercury retrograde can be a very positive indicator. Similar to the periods in infancy where the brain is reorganizing, the nervous system is developing, and very basic communication skills are being refined, between 1975 and 1998 Oprah had the advantage of retracing her steps over territory she had already covered. Her efforts in television broadcasting, film making, and other arenas demonstrated her confidence in herself, and this confidence is reflected in the progressed Mercury retrograding and retracing its steps.

A few days before the Mercury retrograde station, Oprah's Mercury formed a Sesquisquare to her natal Neptune in the tenth house. Mercury made no other major aspect before returning to the sesquisquare by retrograde motion about seventeen days later. Progressed Mercury during the period between 1967 and 1984 marked an intense focus of communication skills with regard to glamour in general, and broadcasting in particular. During this seventeen year period, Oprah moved to live with her father, was selected as Miss Black Tennessee, graduated with a degree in speech communications and theatre, and was selected as the 1986 Woman of Achievement by the National Organization of Women. She had co-anchored the news at age nineteen, anchored A.M. Chicago, which was renamed the Oprah Winfrey Show in 1985 and syndicated in more than 120 cities. She was also nominated for an Academy Award for her role in *The Color Purple*, which opened in 1985.

Sun, Mercury, and Venus Cycles/45

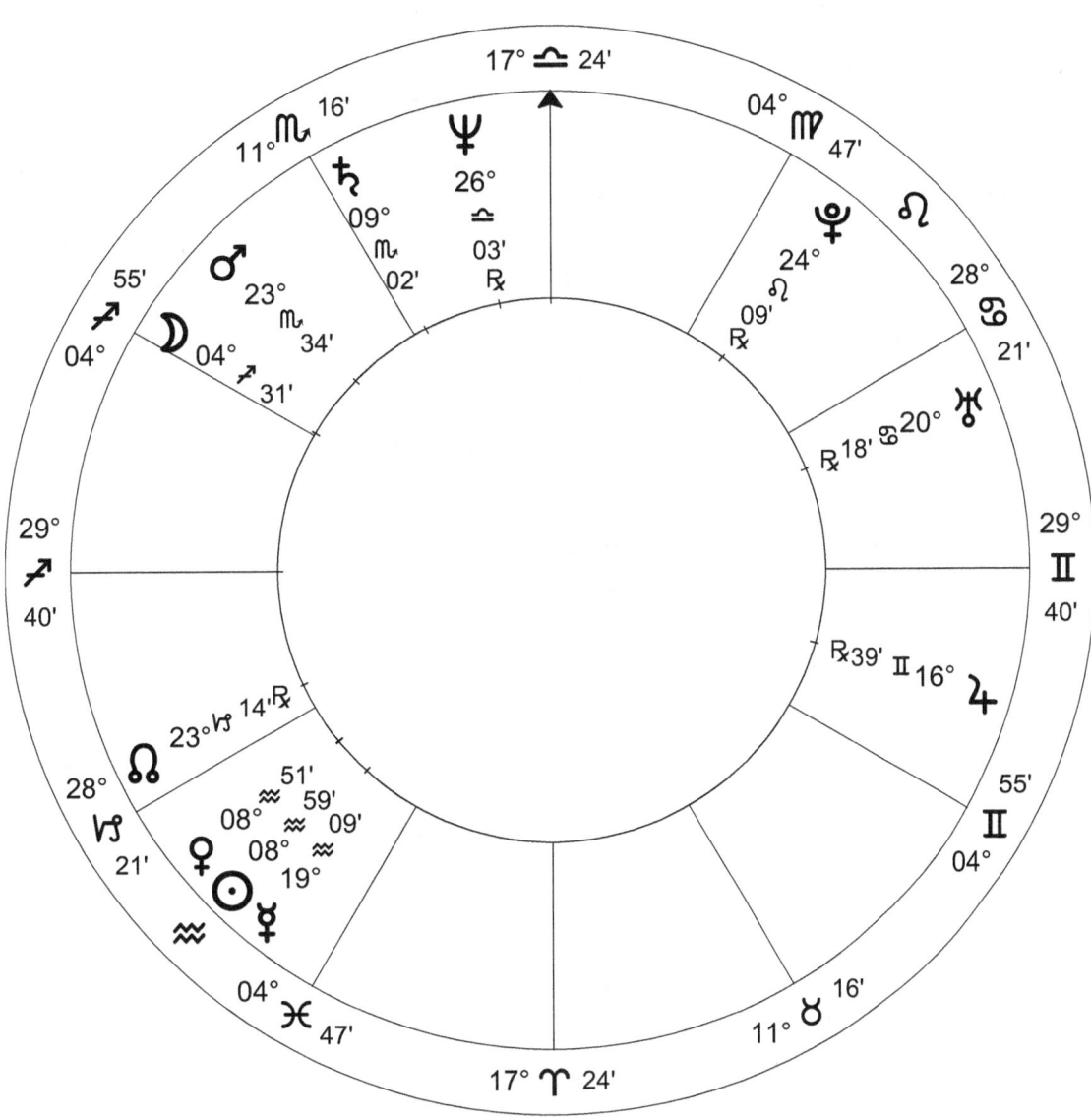

Oprah Winfrey, January 29, 1954, 4:30 am, Kosciusko, MS
Tropical Koch

J. Paul Getty

The son of an oilman, Getty opened his first bank account at age seven, when his progressed Mercury made the direct station. By the time progressed Mercury returned to conjunct natal Mercury, he had made his first investments in oil and was well on his way to becoming a millionaire, which he accomplished at age twenty-three. Within a year of his progressed Saturn retrograde station at age thirty-seven, his father died, leaving controlling interest in his estate to Getty's mother. J. Paul's great wealth came after his father's death and involved oil, real estate, and two hundred affiliated and subsidiary firms.

Summary

This chapter outlines some of the interwoven developmental processes that occur in the first year of human life. The Sun, Mercury, and Venus reflect many of the central themes of infant development, including vitality, physical and mental development, as well as budding social competency. These three planets do not circuit the entire chart by progression, but the aspects they do make are major markers for later development. The rhythm of the three varies from individual to individual because of the retrograde cycles of Mercury and Venus. The richness of the rhythm of the first cycle of transits describes the many variations in infant and early childhood development, and is later reflected in progressed aspects throughout life.

Sun, Mercury, and Venus Cycles/47

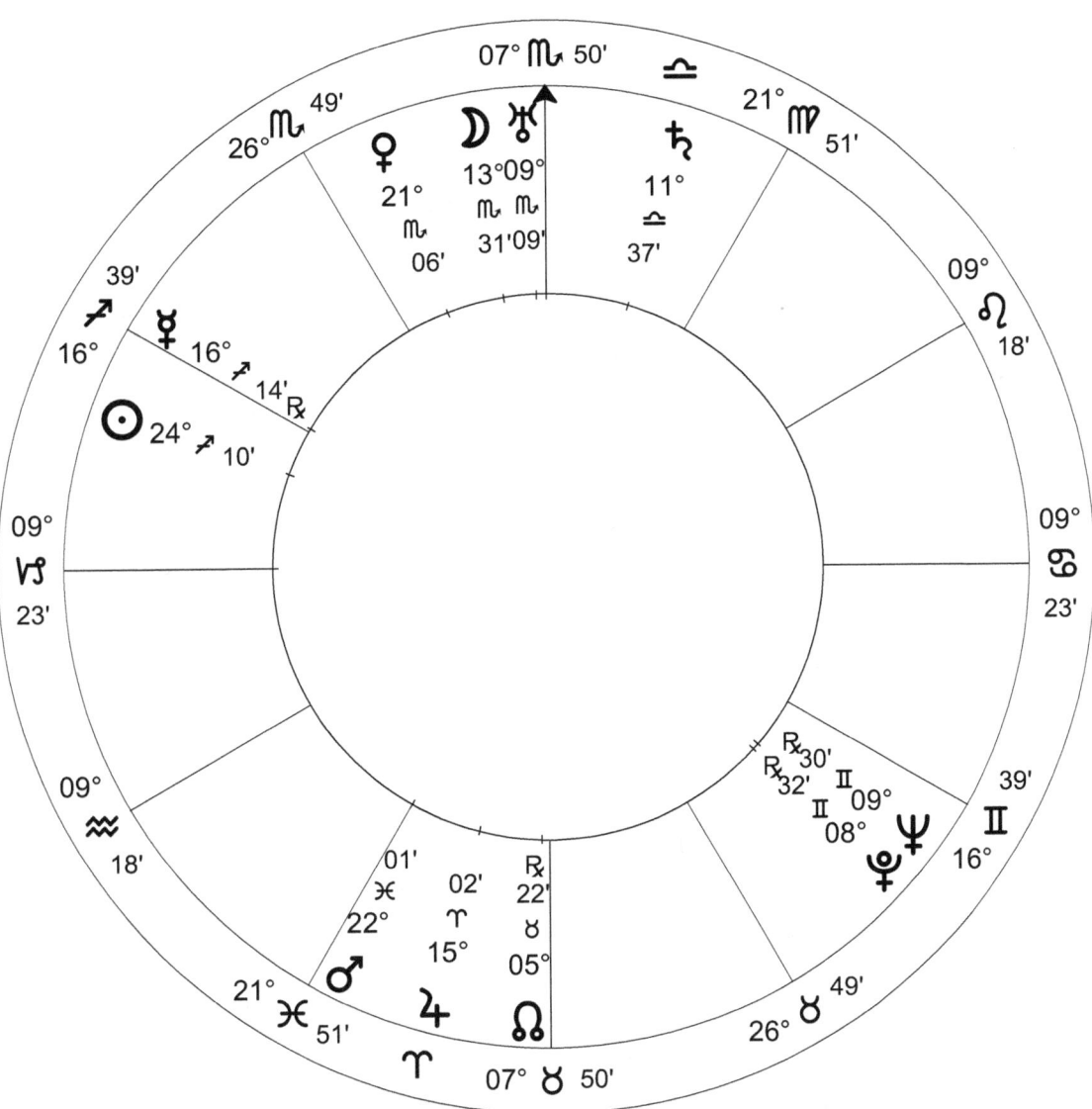

J. Paul Getty, December 15, 1892, 8:43 am, Minneapolis, MN
Tropical Koch

Chapter Five

Mars Cycle

Now we come to the planet that reflects some of the most obvious developmental processes—Mars—the planet is associated with energy and action. Ruperti suggested that Mars is in many ways the agent of the Sun. The Sun indicates the direction an individual is most likely to take, and Mars is "the means of release of [the Sun's] power in outward action and initiative."[9] Mars reflects desire and devotion, impulse and force. As the Sun's agent, it carries the individual from inspiration into active participation in life.

As the representative of action, Mars in its first cycle of about two years provides an indicator of the basic physical and motor development of the infant/toddler. One of the simplest ways for parents to gauge a child's development is to look for anticipated motor skills. As we have seen with the Moon, the Sun, Mercury and Venus, a lot more is going on in terms of brain and nervous system development requisite for those motor skills. Precocity or delay in motor skill development is often the first indication of problems on other levels.

Beyond the obvious physiological indicators, the first Mars cycle is also the imprint of a lifetime. The first two years provide a metaphor that has a robust life of its own. A secure, confident early childhood provides a living model for later athletic activity, mental pursuits, career path, and enthusiastic partnering in romantic and other relationships. The determined, focused effort required in learning to crawl, walk, use the hands, climb steps, and a myriad of other motor activities will be reflected in the capacity to learn to read, to master mathematical skills, climb the ladder to success, and devote oneself to spiritual thought and action.

Esoteric astrology teaches that the capacity for devotion and compassion is shown through Mars. Some of the best uses of action and energy involve helping others, even at risk to the self. Compassion, almost by definition, includes the desire to take action to help others. Consider the task of learning to walk. At the outset this is a largely selfish activity. If you want a toy that is across the room, walking is a really good skill to possess. If you want to keep up with your parents, your siblings, or your friends, again walking is essential. The focus is personal, even the part where you want to please the parent who is encouraging you. It's still pretty much about you.

Any compassionate feelings a child may possess are hard to define at age one or two. Still, the observant person sees the growth of compassion. A two year old picks up a baby's favorite stuffed animal and gives it to the infant, or pats the baby who is crying. Because the first two years of life make an indelible imprint on all future activity, considering the first Mars transit of a chart in this light can provide a framework for a lifetime map of action and devotion.

Mars Developmental Model

The timing of development of motor skills can vary nearly as much as the development of social skills. The timing depends upon the speed of Mars relative to the particular birth chart, and the first Mars cycle depends heavily on the timing of retrograde periods.

Mars makes its first complete transit of the birth chart between 1.88 and 2.17 years (between twenty-two and twenty-six months). This four-month variation is not long in terms of an entire lifetime, and the four month discrepancy is not magnified; that is, the potential time difference does not increase with each Mars return. Depending upon when the retrograde periods occur by transit, there is a developmental blip of sorts. There may be a period when little new activity occurs, but during this time there is a profound consolidation of what has come before. For example, if Mars retrogrades shortly after birth, the infant may not crawl or walk early, but instead may work hard to develop hand-eye coordination. Or the infant may crawl, but show relatively little interest in walking unassisted.

One of my children did not crawl at an early age. I was somewhat concerned, but the doctor said everything was fine—the baby was gaining weight appropriately, and all other indications were normal. One day the baby was grumpy and had a slight fever. The next day he was crawling!

This doesn't sound all that remarkable, but I saw the pattern repeated many times throughout his childhood. He would eat everything in sight for several weeks or months, and then would seem to grow two inches overnight or master some complex task "instantly."

According to Rex Bills' *The Rulership Book*, Mars governs the left hemisphere of the brain, while Mercury governs the right hemisphere.

In the birth chart, Mars aspects reflect the condition of motor nerves and symmetrical movement on the left and right sides of the body, as does Uranus.

Aspects of Mars to its natal position may reflect delays in any of the commonly accepted milestones for motor development (sitting, creeping, walking, etc.).

Mars Development in the First Cycle

This section outlines some of the developmental tasks of infancy and early childhood that are most appropriately associated with Mars. To make sense of these, it may be helpful to keep in mind a few keywords for Mars: energy; desire, competition, action. Although competition is not a big part of early development, I include it here to suggest that the pattern that is laid down during the first Mars cycle will reflect in the capacity to compete later in life.

Note that the developmental processes in this and other tables throughout the book are derived from child development resources listed in the bibliography. Child development coincides with the phase aspects of the planets in remarkable ways, and this is a profound confirmation of the validity of astrology. Don't panic, however, if a child is not right on schedule. The variables are numerous, and children each have their personal developmental rhythm.

Mars Developmental Indicators

0 days: Symmetrical movement and strength indicates balanced development of motor nerves.

57 to 65 days, semisextile: The baby raises the chest without assistance of arms, and turns his head. Touching the cheek elicits a turn of the head toward the touch, in anticipation of nursing.

114 to 129 days, sextile: The baby may purposefully roll over from stomach to back. She holds her head erect and steady. She may start to grasp objects. She raises her head and chest and stretches out her arms. She can raise her head and easily turn it from side to side.

171 to 196 days, square: The baby will bear some weight on his legs, and he can sit without support. He will work to get a toy out of reach, and will object when a toy is taken away.

229 to 258 days, trine: The baby will play ball (probably with little sense of aim) or another simple game. At this stage, playing with a child involves constant going to fetch the ball, handing it over, and letting the child throw it again. You rarely are in the right spot to catch it, but with the kind of practice I associate with trine conditions, the skill level improves. Sometimes the child will be willing to play and sometimes not. Giving him or her the choice is part of the encouragement to develop a sense of self and feelings of confidence and independence, also Mars related traits.

Fear of strangers may occur. This fear may be an early indicator of a sense of separateness at the first Mars square. If the child feels isolated, then the presence of familiar faces is required to maintain a feeling of security. Strangers will simply not be able to provide the same sense of personal safety. While fear is most often associated with Saturn, in mythology it was the sons of Ares (Mars) who instilled fear into the armies at the battle of Troy. Careful attention to early fears helps children to develop confidence in the world, their parents, and themselves.

286 to 401 days, quincunx: The baby is alternately independent and clingy. The adjustment to a happy sense of independence is fraught with tangled emotions. Even though independence is desired, she will remain dependent on the parents for many years to come. The quincunx of Mars offers a time when desire and all the associated feelings can adjust within the psyche. By swinging back and forth between the extremes, she tests the relative safety of independence, and determines a pattern of behavior that feels adventurous and at the same time secure.

As parents, we need to recognize the energetic flow along the continuum of independence, and we need to accept where the child is without pushing for what we want. In this way, the child feels supported whichever way the wind is blowing on any given day. Greater independence is the desired outcome over time, but at this early stage, it's good to take little steps in that direction.

Another development at this time involves the capacity to mimic actions. This ability is essential to a vast array of later learning, and this transition should be applauded. Parents can initiate activities of mimicry, and the child will occasionally initiate them spontaneously. Remember that her attention span is very short. These activities may last as little as seconds or minutes at first.

She will scribble/draw. A chalkboard that can be erased is a great toy, as pictures can be made again and again. A few paper pictures can be saved on the refrigerator. In this way she will see that her efforts are valued. The repetitive nature if scribbling is good for gross motor development, and she will show gradually more refined motor development over the next several years.

343 to 394 days, opposition: The toddler can walk holding onto a hand or piece of furniture. He may walk well, drink from a cup, and play ball with greater coordination. All of these activities are aided by enthusiastic encouragement from parents and others. A cautious infant will need lots of involvement with others to develop these skills. An adventurous child may appear to try harder, or seem more forceful. It's good to keep in mind that the thoughtful infant is watching, and no doubt thinking about walking or other activities even if little action seems to be taking place. Older children in the environment act as a catalyst, as the infant will want to participate in whatever they are doing.

1.1 to 1.3 years, quincunx: This astrological indicator of adjustment can include consolidation of motor learning tasks into more purposeful activity. It could also indicate injuries as the toddler becomes more active. This is a time for parents to take special care to remove dangerous objects from the baby's environment.

1.2 to 1.4 years, trine: The toddler is refining her ability to walk and to feed herself. She may fall down frequently. She can undress herself, and she jumps up and down, scribbles, and stacks blocks. When "reading," she flips through a book rather than going page by page.

1.3 to 1.6 years, square: At this stage, parents may need to discourage biting and hitting. Some skills seem to be forgotten. The child's appetite varies, with days where little is eaten and ordinarily preferred foods are refused. His behavior becomes more unpredictable. He uses the word "no" for everything. He understands himself and shows the beginnings of independence.

A central connection has been made in psychological research between the development of self-recognition and the capacity to predict and then satisfy the needs of others. At eighteen months of age the sense of self-recognition bursts onto the scene in a very Mars-like way. Researchers using mirror recognition tests have established that before eighteen months, the image in the mirror is viewed as more of a social "other" than as the self, whereas at eighteen months, the child grasps the fact that the reflections is of him or herself. [10]

The implications of psychological studies can be applied to the Mars cycle very easily. Showing a toddler a mirror from time to time and talking about who is in the mirror will make the connection more real. The child may seem very interested in the image in the mirror, but clearly not seeing that image as the self. Yet the child will recognize the reflective quality of the mirror, and will look behind her to see a person who is approaching in the mirror. At the second Mars square, these pieces of the puzzle snap into place, and self-awareness is the result.

1.4 to 1.8 years, sextile: The toddler imitates others, especially older children, but she also wants to initiate activities that are familiar. She explores spaces and is gaining a better sense of balance.

1.7 to 2 years, semisextile: Given the span of time when this aspect can occur, I am moved to mention here that growth and development are not without their painful side. For the two year old who is well ahead of his or her peers in development, there is a growing sense of competence, but also a feeling of exposure that can instill caution. Most of us do not thrive by being out in front all the time. On the other hand, the child who lags behind developmentally seems to suffer from the inability to participate equally. However, being a follower has the advantage of providing a lot of second-hand experience, and when a child can pay attention, this is a very valuable learning tool. Either way, your child benefits at this cycle.

1.9 to 2.2 years, conjunction: The toddler can place shapes on a matching board. He climbs stairs with both feet touching each step. He can throw and kick a ball without falling down. He can pedal a tricycle and dance to music. He uses a spoon to eat. He stands and walks on tiptoe. He imitates what others are doing. He loves to re-read favorite stories. He has achieved half of his adult height, and has achieved massive neurological development.

Progressed and Transiting Mars

To experience a triple Mars conjunction to natal Mars by progression, one would have to be born just before the Mars retrograde station. Given the length of time between stations, this is a fairly rare occurrence. Progressed Mars typically forms a semisextile at about thirty-eight to forty-five years of age, the semisquare at about fifty-eight to sixty-two years, and the sextile at about seventy-eight to eighty-two years. These periods will be especially intense when they coincide with other major transits or progressions.

The transits of Mars generally are timed so that Mars will make three passes to conjunct its birth position about every sixteen, thirty-two or forty-seven years. Occasionally there will be one such conjunction and then a gap of seventy-nine or eighty years until the next one. Depending upon when you were born in respect to the Mars retrograde cycle, you could experience several triple transits of Mars to conjunct its own position during your lifetime, and these particular Mars conjunctions will be more intense than single passes, providing you a special opportunity to learn about energetic renewal in your life. Depending on the length of life, you might not experience any triple passes of Mars in conjunction with your birth Mars. However, you will experience Mars retrograde periods with respect to other planets.

Examples

Example One: An individual born in January 1977 experienced the only triple transit of Mars to her birth Mars during 1986. This was an especially problematic year, with events involving people outside the family that caused her and her family members a great deal of anger that resurfaced more than once.

Example Two: Katarina Witt won all of the world and Olympic championships between 1984 and 1988, except for the World Championship in 1986, which she lost to Debi Thomas. Katarina experienced a transiting triple conjunction of Mars to her birth Mars in 1986, perhaps indicating a bit too much energy for her to manage that year. During this transit, Mars was moving relatively slowly, whereas Katarina was born with a relatively fast Mars. She might have won the World Championship that year if she could have slowed down her training pace and managed the excitement better. Debi Thomas had Mars conjunct her birth Mars in December 1985. With that Mars milestone behind her, she was able to settle into her training program more comfortably than Katarina.

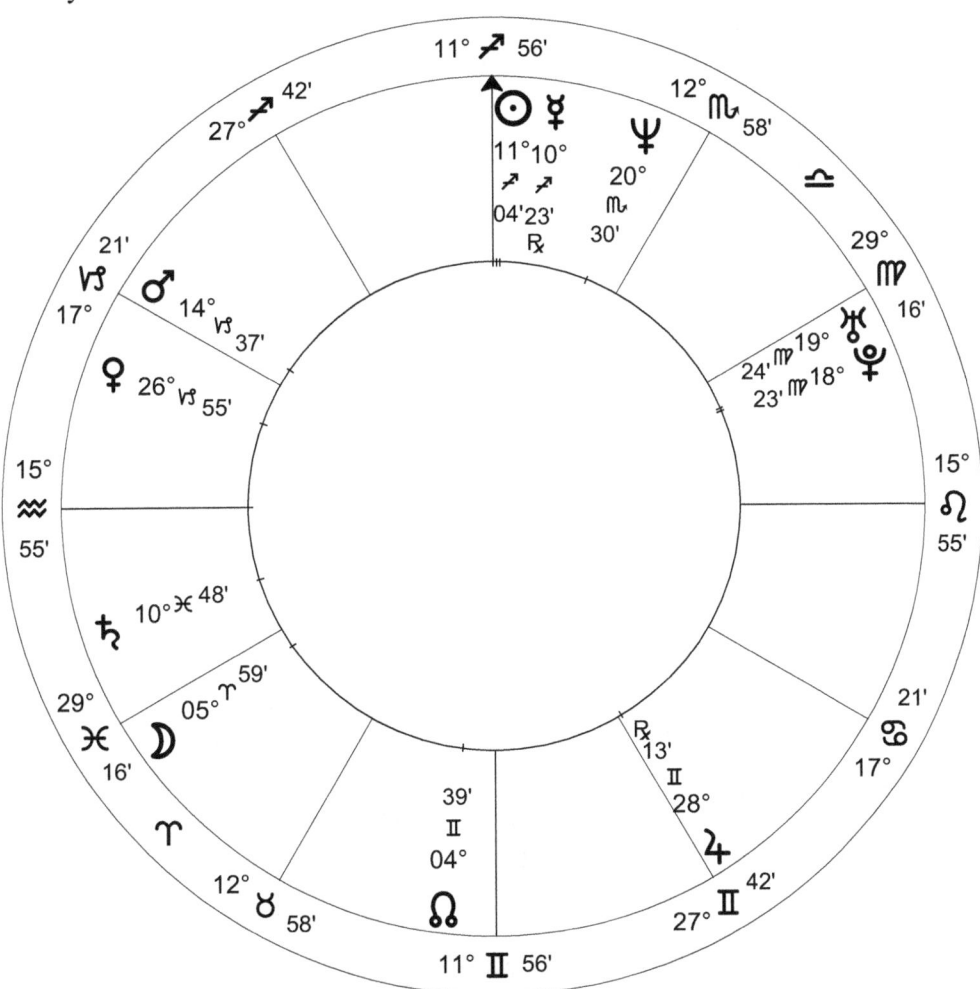

Katarina Witt, December 3, 1965 12:00 pm, Berlin, Germany
Tropical Koch

56/The Astrology of Development

Example Three: Debi Thomas has a retrograde Mars in her birth chart, and her progressed Mars doesn't turn direct until 2028. We have seen that retrograde planets in the birth chart often indicate areas in which the individual experiences a very thorough growth or learning cycle. Debi's skating career and her career as an orthopedic surgeon both indicate her mastery of the energy reflected by Mars. The retrograde birth Mars may have indicated some developmental delay during the first sixty days of her life, but it also indicates the concentrated use of energy reflected in her skating and medical careers.

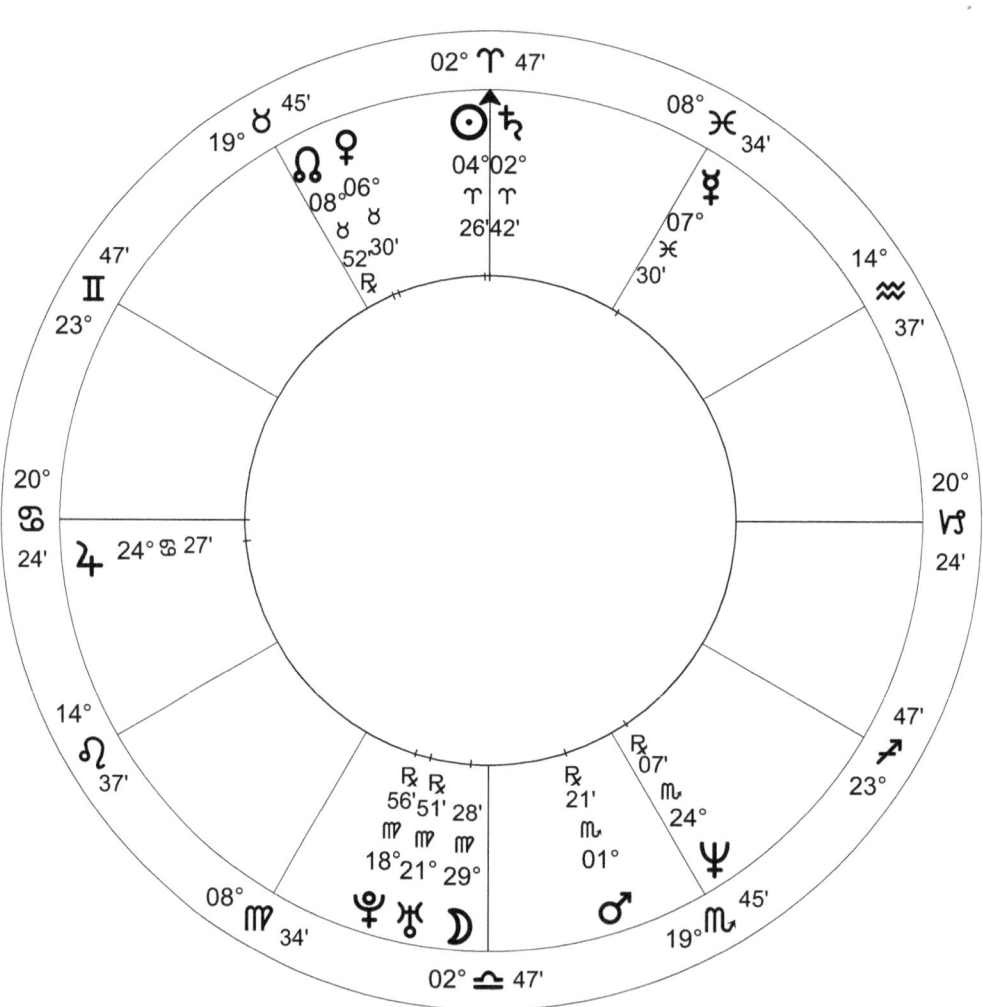

Debi Thomas, March 25, 1967, 12:00 pm, Denver, CO
Tropical Koch

During the 1986 U.S. Nationals and Worlds, Debi's retrograde (and therefore slower) Mars was paced by a slower transiting Mars. The situation was perfect for her; she appeared on the national and international skating scene and skated magnificently. She remembers the 1986 U.S. Nationals as the best experience of her skating career.

Summary

Mars, symbol of energy, represents a double-edged sword in astrological charts. I am reminded of two aphorisms: "Enough is too much," and "Too much is never enough." Which way Mars plays out depends to a very great extent on the temperament of the individual, as indicated by the personal planets, Ascendant, and Midheaven. The first two years of life provide a metaphorical depiction of later Mars cycles. The Mars retrograde cycle is significant for two reasons. First, it pays a major role in charts of individuals born with Mars retrograde, indicating the pacing of their lives. Second, transiting Mars retrograde, relative to the birth Mars, can significantly impact that year in an individual's life. It will be important with Mars to consider what other planetary cycles are in play, especially at the times when Mars forms progressed aspects or returns to its birth position by transit.

Chapter Six

Jupiter: Function and Inspiration

"All the world's a stage,
And all the men and women merely players;
They have their exits and their entrances;
And one man in his time plays many parts,
His acts being seven ages."—Shakespeare, *As You Like It*, Act II, Scene 7

The gods of the ancients breathed life into every day. Their stories reflected every aspect of human life. Jupiter and his counterparts in mythologies from around the world reflected the process of interactions of all kinds.

The gods and goddesses are crazy by human standards because they exemplify isolated human functions. None of the gods could survive long as a human being because none of them has a full complement of life skills. Take Aries (Mars) for example. Here is a god whose whole life is consumed with the pursuit of desires. There is nothing practical here. He probably doesn't take time to eat on a regular basis, and he is reckless beyond imagining. He is hot on the trail of whatever he wants at the moment. We all know someone who is like this, and we have seen people crash and burn when they get out of control.

Jupiter, aka Zeus, is the "king" of the gods. In his role as supreme commander, he has to negotiate between other deities who each are on their own particular rant. He has to settle disputes, yet he causes his own share of mischief as he pursues consorts with the creative tenacity of a bull, a swan, and a human. He has to inspire the gods and humans to be their very best. Jupiter stands between a pantheon of gods and goddesses on the one hand, and the world of humanity on the other. He moderates behaviors of both groups. In the astrological chart, Jupiter reflects the role of wisdom in individual development. "Learn or burn," Jupiter might say to Mars.

Historically, gods in various cultures who are similar to Jupiter were sometimes solar deities who became associated with the planet Jupiter's qualities. The esoteric astrology of Alice Bailey designates both the Sun and Jupiter as planets of love and wisdom. Many of the gods and goddesses associated with Jupiter demonstrate compassion, creativity, and nobility. Many are the protectors of the people in the respective cultures. Some are considered to be the ancestors of human royal families. Some are the source of agricultural plenty. According to Bailey, "The work of Jupiter is to develop these two qualities—mind and love—and bring them into synthetic interplay. Eventually there has to be the complete fusion of love and mind. Jupiter gives an inherent tendency to fusion that nothing can arrest. The achievement of ultimate synthesis is inevitable and something Jupiter promotes. Jupiter in its lowest aspect gives the fulfillment of desire and satisfied demand, whilst in its highest Jupiter is the outgoing expression of love, which attracts magnetically to itself that which is desired."[11]

According to Alexander Ruperti, Carl Jung "relates the Jupiter function to the persona, which is the compromise between the individual and society."[12] While I generally associate the Ascendant with the persona, or what a person reveals to the world, I also agree with Ruperti's assessment of Jupiter. How we function in the world, balancing personal demands against the demands of society, can be delineated by examining the placement and aspects of Jupiter in natal charts, progressions, and transits.

For me, the Ascendant is the mask of the persona, and Jupiter reflects the process of interaction between individual and society. The Jupiter milestones occur every twelve years, and mark moments in the completion of one sort of societal relationship and the commencement of another. Ruperti calls this process the "rhythm ... of an individual's attempt to grow toward being 'more than the an individual.'"[13]

As discussed elsewhere in this book, it is the nature of planetary cycles that the first cycle has the most profound impact on the individual, and that additional cycles emphasize the experience that has gone before. All things being equal, an individual will experience constructive, forward development with each succeeding revolution of a planet. The quotations from Shakespeare throughout this chapter remind us, however, that the cycles of Jupiter first carry us forward toward adult capabilities, then eventually carry us to the end of life, when we lose the physical senses and approach death.

Jupiter, the Giant Planet

So just how big a deal is the god Jupiter? If the size of the planet is any indication, the god is quick and massive. Jupiter's diameter is eleven times that of the earth and its mass is nearly 318 times that of earth. In some ways Jupiter is much faster than the earth. A Jupiter "day" is nine hours, fifty-five minutes, and Jupiter's moons whiz around this huge planet much faster that earth's moon. On the other hand, the Jupiter "year" is 11.86 earth years. Aside from the Sun, Jupiter represents over two-thirds of the total mass of the planets, asteroids, and other objects in the solar system. Jupiter's magnetic field is so large that the tail sometimes encompasses the planet Saturn.

The Spirit within Each of Us

You will see within this discussion of Jupiter a basic outline of human life. While each milestone marks a time to focus on specific issues and processes, you will notice that the cycles are not self-contained capsules. The many processes ebb and flow throughout our lives, reaching individual peaks around the time of each Jupiter return. We sometimes leap ahead of ourselves or lag behind in development, and we are constantly weaving together different needs, desires, and beliefs into the fabric of our lives.

Jupiter is the planet that indicates the Higher Mind in our lives. It shows where and how we seek to develop a more idealistic or philosophical attitude, and where we are able to direct our faith. By the same token, Jupiter shows where we can be impractical, excessive, or ostentatious. Generally, though, we are able to see the big picture where Jupiter is concerned. Jupiter is often associated with the legal system, churches, and civil servants. On a practical level Jupiter governs function, the way things work. This includes processes in the physical body.

Jupiter's First Passage through the Natal Chart

As we have seen with the faster moving planets, the first transit through the chart is extremely important to the developmental processes. The cycles of Jupiter and the outer planets are far longer in duration, and therefore we can expect unique developmental events to continue throughout our lives, regardless of the age we attain. The following represent indicators drawn not from astrological considerations, but from child development texts. Yet we see powerful correlations between the Jupiter cycle and observations of doctors and psychologists.

Conjunction, birth: At birth, each infant is equipped with the capacity for assimilation of nutrients and the associated weight gain. Jupiter reflects liver function, a key factor in assimilation of nutrients, and Jupiter also reflects growth and weight gain in astrological charts.

Semisextile, 1 year: Around age one, a baby demonstrates a characteristic level of confidence when engaging with his or her environment. Even this early in life, a persona is developing, and parents can clearly define the differences in the way their children interact with parents, other adults, children, toys, and other objects.

Sextile, 2 years: The emphasis is on new relationships and the development of communication skills. The key is the power of communication in one's environment. The process of measuring personal needs and desires against the environment outside the body has begun in earnest. The child learns effective, or not so effective, methods of relating to the world, and thereby getting needs met.

Square, 3 years: Here the child faces significant choices. The child chooses the way to go, and then works within the limits of that path. There is concentration of intention. The focus is on action—social skills learned here carry through all future cycles.

Here is an example. A three year old has been the only child in a household for most of his life. A sibling arrives, demanding attention very vocally. The three year old can see that noise gets attention, and may start making a lot more noise than before. This child may even seem to lose social skills because he has never really had to compete for attention before. Now there is a choice: act "grown up" or try to get what you want. For the three-year-old mind, the choice must be intensely difficult, and we see efforts both to please the parents by acting grown up and to meet the desires of the moment by whatever means will work.

A bit of wisdom is usually learned here: you can do both, but you have to figure out the appropriate moments for each as much as possible. When out of the house, you have to act more grown up. When at home, or when the younger sibling isn't around, you can usually get what you need using more grown up tactics. Sometimes, though, you revert to crying, shouting, or pounding on something to get attention.

Trine, 4 years: At this stage, the child usually gathers what has been learned and is willing to take some risks. Sometimes other people can observe that certain values have been absorbed. There is a need to gain self-assurance through practice and through trying new things. This is the age when the question "why" becomes a prominent feature in conversations. The child knows that there are usually reasons for different things, and wants to know what those reasons are.

Quincunx, 5 years: There are adjustments to increasing social activities and introduction to formal schooling. We expect to see evidence of the child's values, and of increasing capacity for teamwork.

Opposition, 6 years: There is often an effort to perfect relationships with other people. The child shows a degree of adaptability in social situations. Ideally there is a more expansive sense of self-confidence. There is a sense of personal power ("I can not only do this, but I can do it well, and I can choose to do it too.").

Often children have an ideal to which they aspire. For example, they may have strong ideas about what they want to be when they grow up.

Children this age can respond to "what if" questions.

Boys are often about six months behind girls in both physical and emotional development at this age.

Some six year olds are able to recognize strangers' faces when they see them for the second time, but this skill may not develop until much later.

Most six year olds can climb, dance, and describe themselves in physical terms.

Quincunx, 7 years: There is a basic understanding of ambiguity. For example, the child knows that mother and father do not always agree, and yet both of them are right to some degree. The capacity to form an opinion is probably in place. At this age children are generally expected to understand the difference between right and wrong, whereas earlier they only understood consequences, and had to ask if something was okay or not.

Children this age understand that certain words have two meanings. This Jupiter moment shares in the nature of Uranus in that intuition is a component of recognizing subtleties of meaning and the nature of jokes. The child also incorporates an understanding of words that are pronounced the same, but have different meanings (spelling may or may not be part of this understanding).

Sesquisquare, 7½ years: With the multiplicity of aspects falling within a short period of time (the Jupiter sesquisquare, the Uranus semisextile, and the Saturn square), there will very likely be stress involved in the developmental process. The child is pulled in three distinctly different directions: to develop an internal sense of self in a social arena, the assimilation of the concept of ambiguity and all its significance, and the emergence of the "I" in the personality with its budding sense of personal authority. Parents can offer extra support when they see signs of stress by explaining ways to handle conflicting information.

Trine, 8 years: After a possible rough patch, by this time the child has a greater capacity to manage interactions with the social system. The basis for moral and ethical values is developed around this age. In addition, there develops the capacity to learn more mature approaches to solving a problem that has already been met in the past. A sense of fairness emerges.

There is a greater understanding of the difference between fantasy and reality. Although children have seen plenty of movies and television by this age, they still may have difficulty distinguishing between fantasy and reality before this time. This point deserves major consideration. After all, if Wily Coyote in Road Runner cartoons lives to see another day after falling off a cliff, whey doesn't Johnny get up and play after falling off the porch? And how come we can see actors after they have been shot and killed in movies, but not someone we know who has died? No wonder younger children have terrifying dreams after watching scary movies!

Square, 9 years: This is a readjustment period. The child measures results of his or her actions, and the moral sense develops further. There may be a choice to be more oneself and less what others want. The second choice may be to set higher or different goals. A third possibility is to contribute spiritually to the world. Social relationships need to reflect the child's higher purpose.

By this age, language skills generally include the capacity to use irregular plurals, such as women and mice, instead of womans and mouses.

Sextile, 10 years: By age ten, the child has chosen a path, adjusted behavior to suit his or her developing sense of ethics and morals, and now reconsiders goals in view of the growing sense of social involvement. There is an opportunity for children to see what they truly want for themselves and for their friends. They seek new horizons in thinking and actions. Group activities now play a part in moving the child ahead in life.

Semisquare, 10½ years; semisextile, 11 years: There may be adjustments in personal relationships. This includes family members, teachers, and friends. This adjustment may be rather painful, and at the same time beneficial.

Conjunction, 12 years: This is the time of coming of age ceremonies around the world. There is a transition from childhood to a more grown up phase. I purposely do not use the word adult here because twelve year olds are not emotionally ready for adult responsibilities. Physically the onset of puberty is a key focus of attention. It is time to assimilate a larger biological and psychological consciousness. This is a time when habits can be changed. It is a time to take the initiative in the area of life where Jupiter resides in the birth chart. Some individuals have moral conflicts at this point. Most feel capable and in control of their lives.

Louis Armstrong

Louis Armstrong grew up in New Orleans under very difficult conditions. By age six he was already performing vocally, and he formed a quartet in 1907, to perform on street corners (at the time Jupiter was transiting his third house opposition his natal Jupiter). Just weeks before his first Jupiter return, Armstrong fired a gun in the street, was apprehended, and sent to a school for black children. While there, he learned to play the cornet. This is a case where Jupiter's cycle coincided with being arrested, something most of us would consider a bad thing. For Armstrong, it was the beginning of his lifelong career in instrumental music.

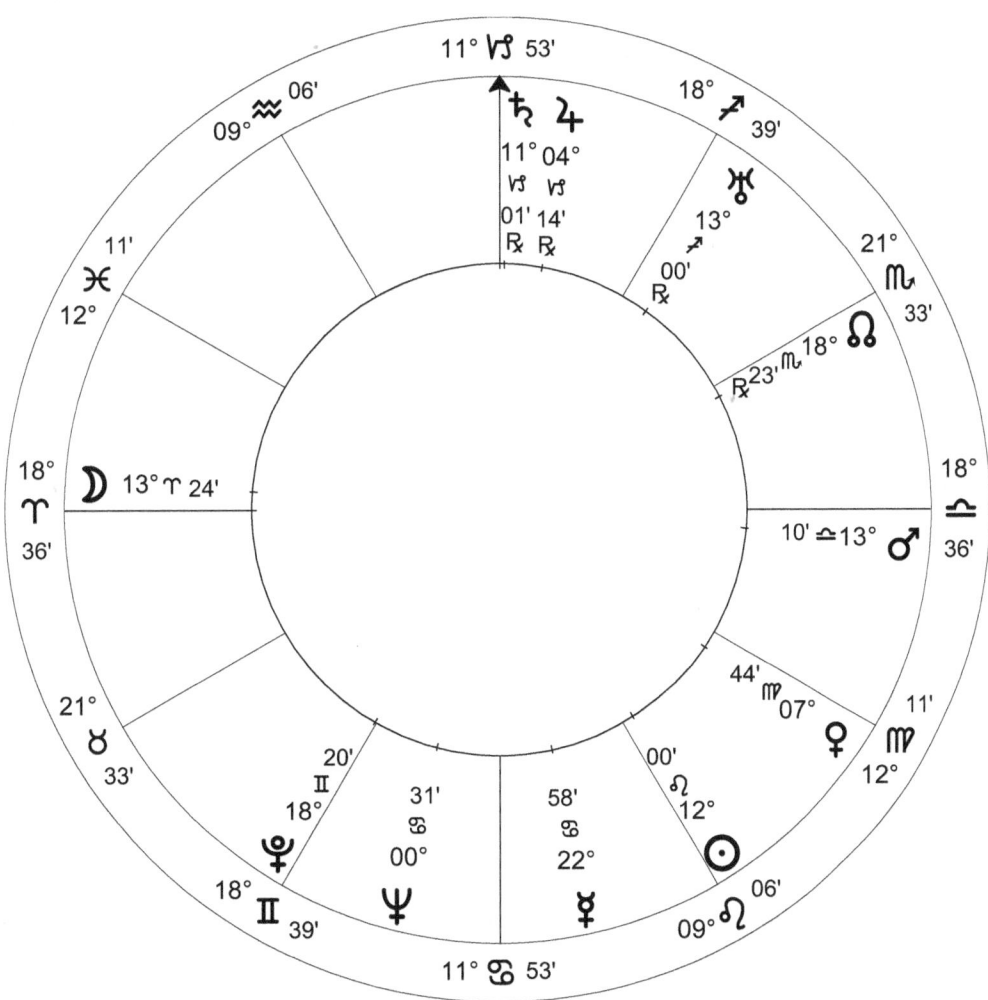

Louis Armstrong, August 4, 1901, 10:00 pm, New Orleans, Louisiana
Tropical Koch

Donald Trump

In stark contract to Louis Armstrong, Donald Trump grew up around lots of money. I didn't turn up many details about his childhood. However, it seems he was "almost expelled from Kew-Forest School in Forest Hills, New York in the second grade for punching his music teacher."[14] This occurrence came at around the time of his second Jupiter sesquisquare, and before the second square. At age thirteen, Donald was sent to the New York Military Academy because his parents hoped "to channel his energy and assertiveness in a positive manner." This move came after the end of his first Jupiter cycle. These two incidents suggest that his first twelve years were exuberant, even excessive in energy and activity.

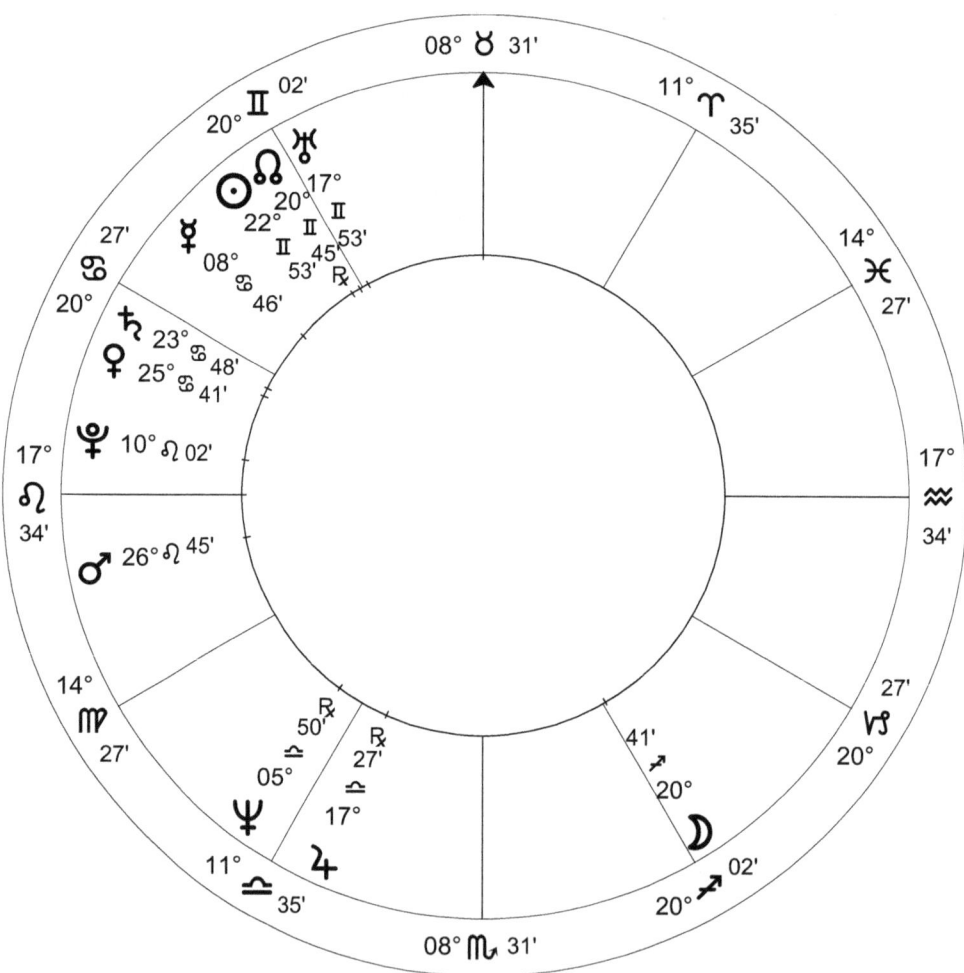

Donald Trump, Jun3 14, 1946, 9:51 am, Queens, NY
Tropical Koch

Summary

Jupiter quite obviously relates to growth of the physical body and the expansion of the mind and heart into intellectual, emotional, and spiritual realms. The several Jupiter returns occurring every twelve years throughout each person's lifetime provide milestones in the adult developmental process that often work in tandem with other planetary developmental markers. Some of these Jupiter influences are mentioned in the following chapters.

Having taken a look at the developmental processes related to Jupiter up to the first return, the next chapter turns your attention to the structural foundations upon which processes rest. At birth each of us has a defined set of potentials. Saturn reflects the significance of developmental processes involving the physical body (bones, skin and teeth to name three major structural factors), mental and emotional development (learning rules, laws and establishing personal beliefs), career possibilities, and a remarkable array of other factors.

Chapter Seven

Saturn: Structure and Time

Saturn, with its magnificent rings and multiple moons, acts as a principal timer of events. Saturn reveals the structure of life from the potential at the moment of birth, through the formative years, the productive period, and into later years, when elders become mentors for the younger generation.

At birth we each have unique potential. Sometimes we will work hard and achieve more. Other times we struggle, only to be frustrated in our desires. Frustrations often teach us greater self-discipline . . . by creating patience, for example. We all have choices along the way. Saturn's birth potential encompasses these general considerations:

- Physical development and health considerations.
- Mental and emotional development.
- Areas of pessimism or limited enjoyment.

- Consciousness of self.
- Career and enduring legacy.
- Life's path in general, from starting point to life lessons to rewards.
- Potential for wisdom and maturity.

One way to summarize the role of Saturn is to consider the capacity for self-preservation. All of the above-listed traits come into play as you seek to defend yourself against perceived attacks, or to go on the "attack" as an assertive, ambitious individual. You develop skills that aid you in becoming a successful, satisfied person. Success depends both on defensive capacity and assertiveness.

These considerations play out in three ways. First, there is the "normal" path—the typical pattern of development that all people follow. Because Saturn moves relatively slowly through the signs, all the people born within about a two to two and one-half year period share many qualities. This path is similar for everyone. Then there is the unique focus you bring to your own life. This is where you reveal your own power and will. This is reflected in the actual Saturn transits you experience, including retrograde periods. The third is based on aspects to and from Saturn by progression and transit. This book considers the first two possibilities: the normal transit of Saturn, viewed from the heliocentric perspective, and the personal experience of the geocentric Saturn cycle.

Following the Saturn Cycle

One method of following the Saturn cycle allows two and one-half years for each sign, beginning with Aries, even if the child is not an Aries. This means that all children, regardless of their Sun signs, display age appropriate qualities of Aries during the first two and one-half years of life, of Taurus in the second two and one-half years, etc. By age thirty, each of us has experienced an infusion of the structured Saturnine qualities of each sign, and is now ready to enter the middle part of life—the productive cycle. During this time we rear children, engage in fruitful work, and develop a presence in the world. Most of us have started productive work before the Saturn return, but this is the period when we deepen our understanding of what we are supposed to be doing during this lifetime.

The unfolding of the Saturn developmental cycle may not correspond to the normal movement of Saturn through the signs. Because of retrograde periods, Saturn may form a thirty degree aspect to its own position as early as age twenty months and as late as age thirty-five months of age. A fifteen month time span at age fifty-five is relatively insignificant in terms of adult development, but this large a difference at age two or two and one half is remarkable—the actual age difference for the first semisextile aspect could be as much as fifty percent of chronological age!

Let's consider the emergence of teeth as an example. The typical age for first molars and canines to emerge is thirty months (about the middle of the time range for the first Saturn semisextile). In primitive cultures, the ability to bite, tear, and chew was critical for survival. A six month delay in developing teeth meant greater difficulty in obtaining adequate nutrition, whereas early emergence of teeth meant the child got a natural developmental boost. A comparable delay at age fifty-six or fifty-eight represents about two to three percent of chronological age. A two percent delay might be reflected in a slow response to a business opportunity or a delay of personal plans due to an event in one's family, but would probably not represent a life-threatening situation.

The First Saturn Cycle

All people begin physical life as helpless infants, and all people eventually leave the physical body. Between these two universally shared events, there are so-called "normal" times for each developmental process to occur. The four major Saturn milestones occur each seven years, four months, and one week on average. In between are twelve less emphatic markers. Some of us are ahead of the curve at each milestone, and some of us fall behind. Astrological timing of development is based upon the average speed of Saturn's motion, compared to what actually occurred for you personally.

Comparison of Heliocentric and Apparent Geocentric Saturn Aspects to Natal Saturn

Aspect	*Geo Date*	*Helio Date*	*Difference*
Conjunction	12-14-1942	12-14-1942	0
Square	08-20-1949	08-30-1949	+10
Opposition	12-20-1956	04-12-1957	+113
Square	03-01-1965	04-26-1965	+56
Conjunction	05-16-1972	05-18-1972	+2

In the above table, the geocentric and heliocentric dates of Saturn aspects from birth to the first Saturn return are compared. In every case, the geocentric aspect occurs before the heliocentric aspect. In each case when there were three transit contacts—direct, retrograde, and direct—the first transit to the aspect was selected.

Comparison of Major Saturn Milestone Dates for Four Individuals

	12/14/1942 Retrograde	02/14/1942 Direct	06/26/1985 Retrograde	10/09/1940 Retrograde
Conjunction	0	0	0	0
Square	+10	+22	+155	-63
Opposition	+113	+161	+142	-64
Square	+56	+378	+249	-107
Conjunction	+2	+344	+38	-57

The data in the second table shows that Saturn was retrograde at birth in three of the charts, and direct in one. In each case, a "+" means that the geocentric aspect occurred before the heliocentric aspect; a "-" indicates that the geocentric aspect occurred after the heliocentric. The numbers show the difference in days. Note that the numbers do not compound during the second or third Saturn cycles, although they may vary within the approximate ranges in the above table.

The main point I wish to make here is the emphatic difference *between* charts. During the first thirty years of their lives, these four individuals either anticipated (+) or delayed (-) what could be viewed as the "normal" Saturn developmental rhythm in their lives. At age seven, a five-month delay is very meaningful, as it could reflect being held back from the start of first grade. Even at age twenty-nine or thirty, an eleven-month difference is substantial. At about age twenty-one, the difference between the second and fourth examples is more than sixteen months! The personal rhythm of the Saturn cycle, then, can be very revealing in terms of physical, mental, emotional, and spiritual development. In the fourth example, where the heliocentric aspects precede the geocentric, one could speculate that spiritual development may have occurred ahead of the normal time, while physical development may have been somewhat delayed.

Recurring Saturn Aspects

Because of the movement of Saturn, similar conditions and feelings occur every twenty-eight to thirty years. Early in life a difference of a few weeks or months can have a big impact on physical, emotional, mental, and spiritual developmental processes. A month seems like an impossibly long time to a six-year-old, while at age sixty a month whizzes by all too quickly. As we have seen with the faster moving planets, an older individual will have gained experience during the formative years, making the second or third transit of a planet more familiar. On the other hand, adult developmental issues when Saturn returns at age sixty or ninety are very different from those experienced at age thirty. Good astrological interpretation differentiates Saturn's transits based on age and other astrological forces that were in play at the time of earlier transits.

Growth—Birth to About Age 30

During the first twenty-eight to thirty years of life, the structure of the physical body develops, mental capabilities expand, emotional changes occur, a sense of values and morals emerges, and work in the world begins. Lasting relationships usually have been formed, and having children may be part of the picture as well.

The demands of the first seven years of life are huge. As we have seen, physical, mental, and emotional development is intense in early childhood. Saturn builds upon the past. From the first breath, the infant is using what happened before birth. The first full transit of Saturn indicates how we each take in familial, social, and cultural information from the environment. Now let's take a look at the major milestones during Saturn's first transit through the birth chart.

First Milestone: About Age Seven

Up to this time, children are primarily part of a close knit family group. The promise of this first milestone is the development of a sense of self. Each child has basic survival skills and steps out of the nuclear family into the immediate neighborhood to meet other children, relate to caretakers outside the household, and begin regular schooling. By this age, most children see themselves as separate from parents and siblings. In fact, around age seven, children may feel somewhat isolated, while also enjoying a new sense of independence.

On the physical level, before this age children know how to climb, and they are usually fairly cautious when climbing trees or ladders. There is enough physical and mental development to allow more fluent handwriting. In addition, children have a clear sense of concrete operations, such as the steps involved in performing specific tasks. The perception of diagonal lines and diamond shapes is gained. Adult first molars and incisors erupt.

Around the time of this milestone, children develop a much better sense of time. They understand the concept of future and past more fully, and may indicate this through fairly sophisticated conversation such as, "I just had a birthday last week, so it will be a long time before I have the next one." This sentence indicates a grasp of before, later, and sequential events. Understanding time may be paralleled by evidence of greater patience.

Mentally the seven year old can remember and repeat sets of five numbers in a row. The concept of differences of opinion is learned. Awareness of the relationship between cause and effect is in place, although obscure relationships will be missed. Children are capable of understanding rather complex jokes, and even make jokes themselves.

A very important transition at this age is the understanding of right and wrong. Individual rules are recognized as part of a systematic structure that can be generalized into a code. Children internalize the "feeling" of rightness or wrongness of their actions, and gradually learn to make their own decisions. While a child of two or three looks to an adult authority figure for information about appropriate action, the seven or eight year old is learning to look within the self for this information.

There is a growing sense of responsibility for personal actions, and also a greater feeling of significance as an individual. Along with self-awareness comes the capacity to question authority of parents and other adults.

Second Milestone: About Age 14 to 15

The teen years are filled with a sense of crisis for most people. Profound physical and sexual changes are in process. Emotions swing from independent, adult assurance to child-like dependence. Undisciplined emotions can lead to rebellion, with disastrous results if a teen does not develop behavioral limits. Defiance, something that younger children are generally afraid of, flares.

Some teens fail to develop the capacity for abstract thought. Evidence is seen in behavior that fails to consider consequences in the distant future, an inability to grasp the principles of logic or geometry, and a pattern of reverting to memorized information instead of working through complex problems. There may be evidence of significant frustration when trying to resolve difficult situations, or a black-and-white thinking style with little capacity for synthesis.

Ideally teens move from primarily inductive thinking toward using the deductive style of reasoning. This provides an opportunity to abandon somewhat unpredictable patterns of thinking and take up a precise, definite, secure mental style. Much of the world seems logical and rational. Critical evaluation ability develops around this age. Abstract thought also develops and benefits from practice.

Unpredictable emotional floods contradict this new style of thinking. Some teens blame others for their difficulties. Parents or immediate caregivers are likely targets for these negative emotions, while more positive feelings are reserved for peers. Expression of sexuality becomes an issue. We all need time to adjust to massive physical changes too. Even though this can be a painful time, it is important to hang out here for a while. For example, rushing into marriage can deprive a teen of the time needed to fully understand changing emotions, physical responses, and mental capabilities.

Even though teens feel grown up and independent part of the time, they still need the support and boundaries provided by parents, teachers, and rules. Saturn reflects the role discipline plays. Around age fifteen, children still need the discipline provided by family and social systems as they gain awareness of social position, intellect and future possibilities.

Third Milestone: Legal Adulthood, Age 21-22

The third major Saturn milestone occurs around age twenty-one to twenty-two. Our society labels us as adults at about this time. Generally this transition is made primarily on the mental level. It is a time when we accept the responsibilities of adulthood; we are legal to drink, vote and marry. At this milestone, it is possible to have a romantic relationship that is not based on peer- or adult-child dependence.

There is a crisis of consciousness. The end of dependence on the parents is more appropriate here than at the previous milestone, when defiance of parental authority often occurs. However, at the third milestone, the individual may actually be more cautious and hesitant about going out on his or her own.

Laws in many states and countries apply this label earlier—at age eighteen, for example. Having the legal responsibility and having the intellectual, emotional, and spiritual understanding of responsibility are two entirely different things. At age eighteen (the Saturn trine or sesquisquare to natal Saturn, depending on retrograde timing), we get to audition for adult status before we have all the mental mechanisms in place to do the complete job. It can be a very tense time, yet it can also be a relaxed period during which adult skills are practiced and perfected.

The transition at age twenty-one is often accompanied by the desire to "go it alone." Students are in college or graduating soon; others have taken jobs and may move away from home. Many have married and begun their own families. They take on the material responsibility for life, and presumably are more thoughtful in their decision-making. They feel alone as they transition from the role of junior family member to the role of adult independence. Even if they marry and have children, they are still going through the transition and may feel very lonely as they make important decisions. Yet they need a separate identity from the peer group just as they needed to separate from the family in order to become healthy individuals.

Fourth Milestone: First Saturn Return, Age 28 to 30

They say that what goes around, comes around, and this is certainly true of Saturn, both literally and metaphorically. The management of earlier experiences definitely affects how each person meets each subsequent challenge. The Saturn return marks the beginning of the most important period of maturity. This is when productive powers are at their height—a time when the individual expresses himself or herself in the world and is able to achieve concrete goals and make a lasting impact. Life turns outward from the self, allowing the individual to meet and interact in the world instead of focusing on internal changes.

Because Saturn has made a full circuit of the birth chart, all possible structural relationships have been formed. This means that all the pieces are in place, for good or ill. For instance, nearly complete physical growth has occurred. During the next twenty-eight to thirty years, physical effort shifts away from growth and toward work and maintenance of health. As the same Saturn phases are repeated, the person benefits from life experience.

Saturn is in the sign it occupied in the birth chart. However, each individual has twenty-eight to thirty years of experience building the structure of the physical body, the mental capacity, emotional tendencies, and spiritual understanding. Thus passage through the second Saturn transit of the chart will be significantly different from the first. At this time people may review the past and get an attitude check-up. Are they accomplishing their material ambitions? Are they on the best career track? What kinds of changes may be necessary or appropriate at this time in order to get moving or keep moving in a positive direction?

The time of the Saturn return is good for clearing out the dead wood of a stagnant career, old relationships, and other things that are no longer useful. This is also a time of beginning. After essential repairs or rethinking, life takes off in a new direction. In addition, deeper roots prepare each person for a successful second twenty-eight to thirty year period.

During the transitional period just before and after the Saturn return, both self- and social-awareness increase. Most people vividly remember the stress of the Saturn return even if they knew nothing about astrology. Sometimes there is physical illness, psychological stress, or a spiritual shift of large proportions. A fruitful approach to this time includes taking full responsibility for one's actions even when difficult circumstances have intervened. We are responsible for how we choose to respond to events even if we have no control beyond our own emotional response.

For the foreseeable future, how we respond to life is what matters most of all. We have the opportunity to choose our associates, choose our career, and choose our belief systems. We are challenged to reach our highest potential in all areas of our lives. We are, of course, building on everything that happened during the first period, finding remedies for gaps in our education or worldview, and forging ahead. If there are difficulties, we find that we not only have to face them, we have to sort out issues from the past as well.

Keep in mind that no one stops being the person represented by the birth chart. However, we all enter an extended period during which we add nuances to our repertoire of behaviors.

Saturn's Minor Milestones (Or Are They?)

Between the major milestones of the first Saturn cycle, there are twelve other points on the path to the first Saturn return, and each of these has its own significant developmental demands. Most astrologers would not identify these intermediate steps on the path as momentous, but they have serious implications for childhood and early adult physical, emotional, mental, and spiritual developmental processes.

Age, Aspect, and Developmental Tasks of Saturn

2.5 years, semisextile: Second molars emerge, and the child is capable of chewing and eating most foods. Canines also emerge at or just after this age.[15]

3.66 years, semisquare: The roots of baby teeth are all completely formed. Children have a lot more imagination about where to go and what to do than their almost four-year-old capacities can manage. They may feel that others are constantly trying to hold them back. Although they get plenty of encouragement in some directions, they feel restrained in others. There may be strong evidence of development of willpower, both for getting things done and for waiting for things to happen.

5 Years, sextile: At this age, baby teeth begin to come out in preparation for permanent teeth. Between now and age seven, the first molars erupt. For most children, beginning school offers an opportunity to develop social skills and to accept a new level of responsibility for themselves.

10 years, trine: At around this age, children develop the ability to remember the faces of strangers (a remarkable "social" skill considering that much early childhood learning involves repetitive practice). They are aware of bodily changes. They may collect things.

11 years, sesquisquare: Bicuspids generally emerge around this age. Impulses that were more instinctive before this time now become more consciously directed. Children can develop and sustain a plan without much guidance. They can take on independent learning projects. Evaluation skills become stronger.

12 years, quincunx: The second molars typically emerge. Pubic hair may develop.

17 years, quincunx: The long bones in arms and legs fuse, ending further lengthening, around age seventeen or eighteen.[16]

18.5 years, sesquisquare: Wisdom teeth may appear, and the time period can vary from around fifteen to twenty years. Some people never develop the third molars. Emotional, mental, and spiritual wisdom all provide focus for activities at this stage. Teens may learn greater patience, for example, especially if they are involved in the care and teaching of younger children.

19.66 years, trine: Individuals identify and understand adult levels of responsibility. This aspect precedes the next major milestone at age twenty-one, when the individual reaches legal adulthood. This aspect marks a period of working with concepts of adult activities and responsibilities, generally without the full weight of economic and social responsibility of adulthood.

24.5 years, sextile: This aspect occurs at approximately the same time as the end of the second Jupiter cycle. People have completed a cycle of intellectual development and now have the opportunity to put what has been learned to work in the material world. Around this time they begin in earnest to develop more sophisticated business and social relationships.

26 years, semisquare: Generally there has been an acceptance of adult responsibilities by this time in terms of employment, completion of school, and social relationships. There may be tension concerning previous decisions, especially if they have resulted in strained relationships.

27 years, semisextile: Comprehensive life skills include consideration of physical, mental, emotional, and spiritual needs and desires. While there may not be a specific event associated with this minor aspect, often people can point to a single lesson they learned around this time, perhaps something that set the stage for the upcoming Saturn return.

Example: Accident Victims

Two women and a man were driving in the same car and were involved in a devastating accident on August 27, 1967. The first, born August 17, 1920, had polio in infancy, and this delayed her walking and possibly other physical development. However, she did learn to walk, and had an otherwise rather normal childhood. She also had an active adult life with her husband and son. In the birth chart Saturn formed a close semisextile to Neptune, suggesting the possibility of paralysis or a growth problem. The Saturn sextile to Pluto indicates a possible underdevelopment as well.

At the time of the car accident, transiting Saturn formed a quincunx to its birth position from Aries to Virgo. The leg affected by polio was severely broken, as was the opposite shoulder, and there were massive bruises. The recovery period was long and painful, with several surgeries. Prolonged immobility may have accelerated the process of osteoporosis, and the same leg was shattered in a later accident, necessitating another prolonged recovery.

The second woman, born November 17, 1944, experienced severe ear, nose and throat infections in early childhood around the time that transiting Saturn was semisquare its natal position. The infections persisted and at the time Saturn reached the sextile, she underwent surgery to remove the tonsils.

In the car accident, she suffered head trauma, including multiple fractures of the jaw that required two surgeries to repair. At that time transiting Saturn was closely square natal Saturn.

In both cases, the injuries in the car accident reflected the early childhood developmental and health issues in that the accident affected the same parts of the body. Most individuals will not ever have such serious accidents, but almost everyone will have events later in life that closely parallel early childhood experience, especially where Saturn is concerned. With Saturn, these events are often more evident than with other planets because Saturn relates to such obvious things as skin, bones, and teeth—concrete things as opposed to mental or emotional processes, or spiritual growth.

Saturn reflects karmic conditions in the birth chart and also by progression and transit. We can thus speculate about the karmic implications of repeating situations and events. What does the individual need to learn and how do the repetitive events help with that learning process? This book does not focus on such considerations, but I want to acknowledge that they are often just as real as the physical side of life's events.

Summary

The first Saturn cycle reflects the structure of development from birth to full adulthood on every level. The structural components of the physical body have definitive connections with Saturn's aspects to its natal position. Direct parallels to physical development can be observed on the mental, emotional, and spiritual levels.

It is worth noting that Saturn milestones tend to be far more evident in the material world than those of the other planets. In considering the stages in the Saturn cycle, especially the major milestones, you can see how the cycles of the faster planets often mesh with Saturn's aspects to form a complex pattern. The physical development associated with Saturn, such as bone growth and emergence of teeth, goes hand in hand with growing social skills, mental activity, emotional maturation, and spiritual awareness.

Chapter Eight

Uranus: Independence and Intuition

"Why am I so wound up and alert?
What does this excess of feeling mean?
What disaster must my E.S.P. avert?
What is the experience I've 'foreseen'?"—From "Intuition" by Lianne Olive Hennig[17]

"Intuition is the source or the bestower of revelation . . . Intuition brings three qualities with its appearance: Illumination, Understanding, Love."—From Alice Bailey, *Ponder on This*

Uranus has a relatively regular orbit, with eccentricity of only about .05 (compared to Mars at .09, and Pluto at .25. This fact, combined with the great distance of Uranus from the earth, tells us that where phase cycles are concerned, everyone experiences the Uranus cycle at nearly the same age, with any deviations resulting from retrograde periods. This makes Uranus a high quality timer in terms of events (measured by transits) and life cycles (measured by the phase cycle of the planet). The psychological impact of Uranus phase cycles is reflected in specific ways:

- Independence. As Uranus makes aspects to its natal position, individuals reach definitive milestones of independence. The first milestone is birth, where the infant is separated from the mother and must manage all bodily rhythms and functions on its own. Each subsequent aspect reflects particular developmental steps toward independence of some kind.
- Perception. The Uranus cycle reflects the natural development of perception on the physical, emotional, mental and spiritual levels. The eighty-four year length of the cycle indicates that perception continues to grow and develop throughout life.
- Intuition. Here is another capacity that develops over time, often deepening into profound psychic awareness in later life.
- Impulsiveness. Most of us are more impulsive in youth, and learn to moderate this tendency with caution and thought. Even in old age, though, what may have been carefully considered by an individual will seem impulsive from other people's perspectives, largely because the internal thought processes are not visible.
- Rebellion. This quality is easier to observe in young people because they have not developed subtlety of style. In older individuals, the above factors affect the appearance of rebellion, if not its actual texture.
- Ambiguity. Ambiguity is one facet of intuition. This is because intuition is a glimpse into the future—insight about what may happen. The future is necessarily vague—we don't know exactly how events will unfold. Prophecy has always been ambiguous for this reason.
- Crisis. Traditionally, when we face a crisis, we attempt to restore the earlier state of supposed normalcy. This is the approach of allopathic medicine, for the most part, and of modern psychology. In fact we measure psychological problems precisely as a divergence from the "norm."

Since we all share the timing of the Uranus cycle, we often view its indicators as "normal." At the moment we experience the changes we feel very strange—possibly alienated from other people—but the fact is that our peers are negotiating the same general developmental hurdles at around the same age. Depending on retrograde periods, the first Uranus square can happen anywhere between ages sixteen and twenty one.[18] As we have seen with other planets, the variations are most pronounced in the first half of the cycle, with different age groups closing the gap as they approach the Uranus return. The age differences at the first square range from sixteen to twenty-one, while at the return the range is fewer than two years. About half of these observed age differences relate to retrograde periods, while the other half relate to the eccentricity of Uranus' orbit.

Eccentric or Progressive?

The Uranus cycle provides a personal means of becoming or creating what your internal response mechanisms demand. You may experience an inner "voice" in your mind, or possibly images on a mental screen. A third possibility is feelings in your physical body that transmit meaning to you. Crises constellate the required factors to propel you into a higher state that is beyond what you might have accomplished as an individual. In this sense a crisis is transpersonal in nature. It demands going beyond one's individual nature.

Many people believe that intuition is nothing more than a combination of very careful observation plus past experience. They believe that we figure out the most likely future turns of events in this way. Actually, intuition is a component of mind that first arises on its own, unbidden. You probably have had hunches that something would happen, and then it did. You didn't ask about what might happen. You just had the flash, seemingly isolated from other mental activity.

Because intuition is a part of your mental apparatus and because mind can be trained, intuition can be trained, or at least you can practice allowing intuition to come. Over time you become better at noticing intuition at work. You still may not be able to just sit down and say, "Okay, now I'm going to be intuitive," although some people do achieve this level of ease.

The examination of Uranus in this chapter focuses on your natural intuitive potential. It tracks the movement of Uranus through the heavens, stopping to consider what is occurring each time Uranus reaches a significant distance from where it was in your birth chart.

Your path is truly your own. That means that Uranus and its transits only point out the likely pathways, not the particular turnings your life will take or the choices you will make. It shows where and when you may be jolted out of complacency and sent in a new direction with a new resolve.

As soon as you are born, as soon as you draw a breath, you are an independent human being. You need years of care to grow into an adult, but you are essentially complete at birth. Your intuitive potential was also in place when you were born. Because your mind was not very organized, and because you had very little sense of boundaries, it would be highly unusual for you to recall any instances of intuition from your earliest years. However, your parents and people around you may have suspected that you had a pretty good grip on what was going to happen, at least in the immediate future.

Here is an example of intuition at work in very young children. Their father is a fireman. He usually, but not always, works one day on and two days off. This means that every third day their father comes home from work in the morning before the normal time for his small children to wake up. However, both children are typically awake a few minutes before their father opens the garage door, and it is clear they know he is coming, even though there is no obvious way for them to know. Even if he comes a bit earlier or later, the same thing happens—they wake up a few minutes before the garage door opens. What awakens them? An intuition.

Now let's look at how intuition naturally interfaces with your other abilities and talents. You will notice that some of these connections (aspects to other planets and points in your chart) will seem completely natural to you, while others may not ring any bells right away. There may also be some apparent conflicts that require effort to resolve. Because Uranus and the other outer planets move so slowly, you share some of these connections with all the people born close to your birth date. Because of long retrograde periods, these dates are only approximate.

Semisquare, First Uranus Milestone: Clarifying the Mind, Age 9 to 10

At around age ten, you reach the first Uranus milestone. This time is often stressful, as you are moving from childhood toward becoming a teen. You are growing very fast, and your mind is expanding into all sorts of new territory. One of the things you learn to do is forecast outcomes of your actions. At this time you develop an internal sense of what to do. You begin to make decisions based on what "feels right" to you, regardless of what you think your parents might say.

This milestone occurs in the midst of the period during which the conscious ego is being built and strengthened. The development of active self-expression also occurs here. Intuition, although not consciously cultivated, becomes an active part of problem-solving strategies.

Square, Second Uranus Milestone: Centering Your Self-Awareness, Age 18 to 20

Your basic emotional and mental capacities are developed by the time of this milestone. Sexuality has developed, as have the desire for friendships among your peers and a sense of your place in your social circles, religion, and the institutions around you. You reach out from your family to embrace the world.

This is a challenging time in your life. If the passage of the first milestone brought you greater confidence, then you face these challenges with an open mind and heart. If the first milestone was especially tough, you enter this new phase of your life cautiously, taking careful steps to avoid any setback. You may even be overly cautious.

Sesquisquare, Third Uranus Milestone: Insight into Career and Associates, Age 29 to 30

This milestone often coincides with the first Saturn return, another type of milestone in your life. At this time you choose your associates and establish a means of social participation. There is agitation; you may be pushed to become more independent of family and culture and to choose your own direction in life. You also may feel that you still have not completely resolved the challenges you met at the last milestone.

At this time you gain a broader perspective of your life. Your intuition tells you that the future is there waiting for you. Your life experience tells you that you have come through previous challenges. You conclude that you are capable of dealing with what life offers, and that you don't have to do everything right this minute, although you may feel an urge to do so.

Opposition, Fourth Milestone: Peak Productive Period, Age 39 to 42

At this time you have reached the peak of your productive cycle. You have constructed your life, family, and career, and you may have left romantic and business partners behind. More importantly, you have constructed a self-image. By this time attitudes have crystallized to a large degree. You have greater awareness of what you must do, in contradistinction to what society dictates that you do. You may face a deconstruction of the self-image, with upsets in family, career, and social life. Or this can be the beginning of construction of your true individuality.

Notice the word "beginning." Far from being the end of your growth and development, this milestone marks an awareness of the future direction of your life. This is an ideal moment to pay attention to your intuition. You can get an especially strong indicator of the future direction of your life and use that information to make an impressive first step in the direction your heart most strongly desires.

Sesquisquare, Fifth Milestone: Examination of Your Life, Age 50 to 52

This milestone occurs during a period of potential healing in your life. You have come full circle with many of the problems that arose in childhood or early adulthood, and now you are able to make the most of what you have experienced. There is a profound concentration and meditation on what can be considered to be a completed structure. Identification with some part or the cosmos results in an expansion of consciousness.

Many people start a new life around this time. There is a revision of one's attitude toward intimate family members and friends. If the previous milestone resulted in a creative burst, then this milestone represents a continuation of that cycle and a branching in new directions suggested by your individual healing and creative processes.

Square, Sixth Milestone: Detachment from the Past, Age 61 to 62

At this milestone and in the following ten year cycle, you experience detachment from the goals of the productive cycle. You may retire from the career you pursued during much of the previous productive cycle. If the previous milestone involved significant change, you find that you focus on spiritual matters in a new way. If no changes were made, then further crystallization of beliefs occurs, and this can become quite painful if there is friction with your associates.

Intuition can arise like a thunderbolt, showing you how to gracefully change from dynamic production to subtler management and instruction tasks. Mentoring becomes a logical alternative to previous leadership activities.

The intuitive challenge of this milestone is to anticipate changes well in advance, thereby being prepared for most eventualities. You may find that you anticipate events and the associated emotions. Within the ebb and flow of events, you sense an important new rhythm in your life.

Semisquare, Seventh Milestone: Intuitive Integration, Age 72 to 75

Life's dharma has been resolved by this time, to a great degree. A new sense of fulfillment results, along with a sense of wholeness. You can become a teacher or mentor for younger people. There is a sense of summing up your life and work. The focus is deeply internal and may cause some stress. It is appropriate to think about the end of life and preparation for the afterlife, although you may not be all that close to the actual end.

Conjunction, Eighth Milestone: Contemplative Actualization, Age 83 to 84

At this point wholeness has been demonstrated and Unity is perceived. There is a kind of initiation that leads to a new level of restored vision. Mundane details are best handled by someone else, as you generally don't care that much about them any more, and may not be as capable of fulfilling obligations as you once were. Much time is spent in contemplation. Changes made at previous milestones strongly influence individual direction at this point in life. There is a symbolic climax in soul growth, although further growth continues until the end of life.

Examples

A woman with Uranus in the first house and ruling the Midheaven had the following Uranus milestone events:

- Semisquare, first volunteer work.
- Square, engaged to marry.
- Sesquisquare, moved three times.
- Opposition, engaged to marry (second marriage).
- Sesquisquare, moved across the country to take a new job.
- Square, received a diagnosis leading to major surgery.

His Holiness Karmapa

From the perspective of Uranus, we notice that at the time of His Holiness Karmapa's twenty-first birthday, a very significant moment in his spiritual life, transiting Uranus is within a half degree of the sextile to Uranus. This timing is not unusual. The twenty first birthday has marked the legal transition to adulthood in countries around the world, and it parallels the course of Uranus astrologically.

Saturn formed a tredecile aspect at the time of this birthday. While most astrologers would not consider that aspect, for the Karmapa it is a profound indicator of the depth of his spiritual ca-

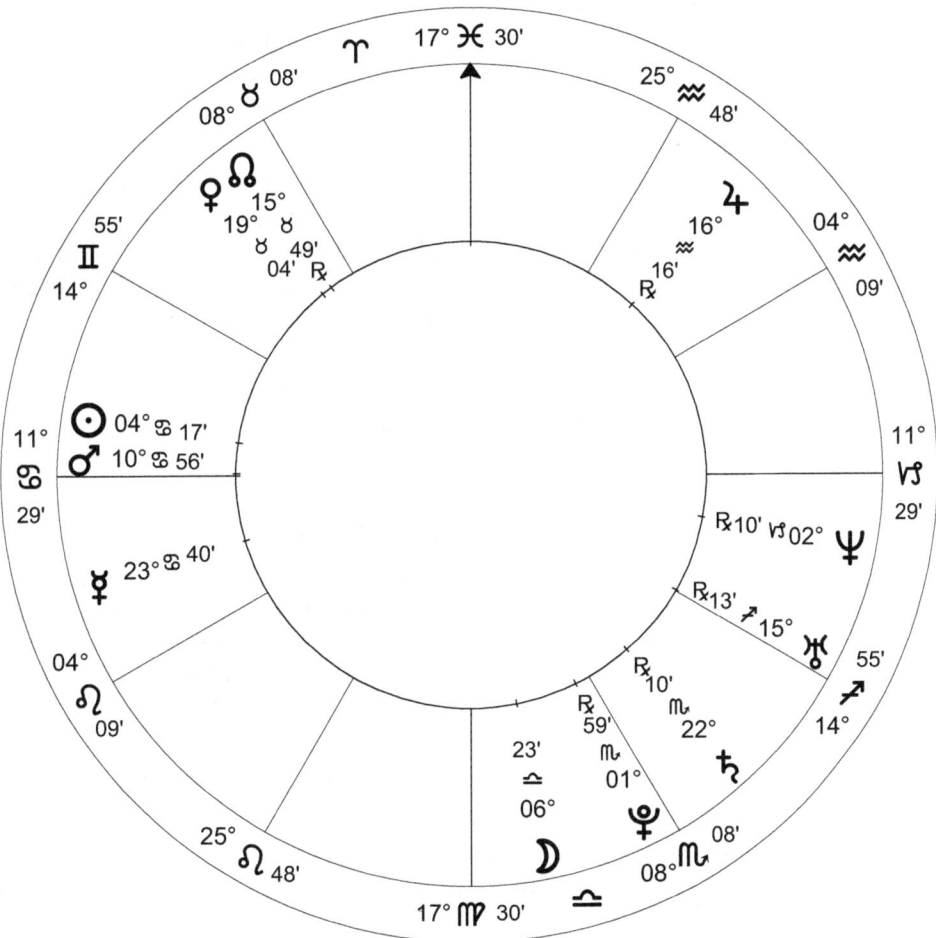

H.H. Karmapa, June 26, 1985, 6:44 am, Barkol, China
Tropical Koch

pacity. The Karmapa is one of very few individuals who are thought to have transcended the boundaries of time; these lamas recall their past lives, recognize items that belonged to them then, and relearn vast quantities of religious text in one reading. The Karmapa has living teachers who knew him in his previous lifetime, and he recognized some or all of those teachers upon meeting them for the first time.

The outer planets often have little impact in people's lives, or at least little visible impact. I believe this is true because many people cannot or do not allow themselves to relate to the world through extrasensory means. Uranus, for example, allows a person to see what is happening right now, or to see the materials available right now, and to understand what may happen in the future, or what those materials may be used for in the future. Most of us can predict what food will taste like, based on the list of ingredients, but sometimes we are fooled. Many people are adept at using tools for purposes other than the original design. These are basic ways we use Uranus.

I have met a few individuals who are very skilled in forecasting (without the benefit of astrology, I might add). This could involve their work, or future events for family members, or future plans for themselves. These individuals are drawing on the energy reflected by Uranus in the birth chart. Often they have thought about things for some time before they gain specific insights. Other times the insight comes almost instantly when a situation arises. The intuitive style depends on the individual; the energy is a reflection of Uranus in the birth chart.

In the case of the Karmapa, the energy of Uranus is vividly reflected in his life, his decisions, his poetry, and his actions. It will be interesting to follow the course of his life as he approaches his first Saturn return, and on into his later adult life.

How to Benefit from the Energy of Uranus

A fundamental purpose for the kind of energy Uranus represents is equilibrium. As rattled as most of us are by the sudden events associated with Uranus, the fact is that those events are generally instrumental in bringing us back into equilibrium in some area of our lives. Each Uranus milestone presents this energy in a different light, and we can assess that difference through the nature of the aspect involved.

Let us reconsider the first Uranus milestone at about age ten. This is a time that adults can actually become rather complacent about children. The kids are no longer small and powerless. They can think problems through. They can generally be depended on to take care of their basic physical needs, and they also help around the house, can handle grocery shopping, and function in a wide variety of social situations.

Yet the aspect is a semisquare, and a basic definition of this aspect includes words like tension, stress, internalized thought processes, and anxiety. Ten year olds may often think they are not strong enough, smart enough, or emotionally tough enough to get through each day alone. At the same time, they are told to grow up, act like adults, handle their own problems, and be more independent. These thoughts and self expectations are a formula for disaster for the child who is not so grown up or confident.

An astrologer may be able to help the child and the parent by providing information about the timing of this transition, the general nature of what to expect, and options for each person for those really tense days. Parents can help kids create a set of cues so they (the parents) know when to step in with some help. Here is an example: When my daughter was this age, she went through some very tough experiences. Some years before, we had developed a habit of always shopping together for her shoes. No one else did that. We would hang out at the mall, walk up and down, try on shoes, eat pretzels, and just talk. When she was age ten, I realized that sometimes she would say she needed new shoes when what she really needed was the walk and the talk. It became a private joke between us! When she was out of sorts, I would ask if she needed new shoes, and we would laugh, and then go shopping, just the two of us.

Summary

Each Uranus transition in your lifetime will be the first time you experience the transit, at least until you are quite old. For the topics mentioned at the beginning of this chapter—independence, perception, intuition, impulsiveness, and rebellion—you will have experiences throughout your life that are "first time" events. You will continue to be surprised by the intensity of these experiences, even though you have lived through many reruns of the phase aspects of other planets.

Keep this "first time" feeling in mind when you look at the charts of clients. Not only is the experience the first time for them, they don't even associate the events in their lives with the cycles of the planets. They may have a hard time grasping the concept at all. What they will benefit from is basic explanations of what the milestones or transitions bring into people's lives in general, and a look at how those generalities match up to their personal experience.

You, as an astrologer, can match up the cycles of the different planets to provide a sort of calendar of experience. You can also tell the client when a particular effect will begin to be felt, and when it will be past. Often, clients get great benefit from simply knowing that they are not crazy, they are not stuck in whatever dreadful experience they are having, and that there will be an end at a specified time, a moment when they will begin to feel better, or at least different.

The map of the Uranus phases is one that portrays events that occur on the inner plane of existence as well as in the material realm. Many people experience no outward signs of what religions call "inward, spiritual grace." These people grow and learn without the external trauma to mark the events. Others have major events, with the Uranus cycle marking wildly exciting or devastating accidents and incidents that pinpoint the planetary cycles definitively.

In the next chapter we turn to Neptune, a planet that doesn't shock us into equilibrium the way Uranus sometimes does, but instead dissolves the boundaries we have created and the fears we may have nurtured.

Chapter Nine

Neptune: Paradox and Dissolution

Neptune, according to Ruperti, dissolves "those Saturn limitations and fears by exposing one to the glamorous dreams and visions of some sort of mystical transformation."[19] He goes on to say that Neptune shows an area of life where matters become unfocused because Neptune's role is to dissolve any rigid boundaries we have created through the auspices of Saturn and Jupiter.

The cycle of Neptune indicates the timing of events and conditions that bring unfamiliar ideas and things into one's life. These are times when we desire or aspire to things we can't even know. Certainly some of us have succumbed to the attraction of alcohol and drugs to carry us into realms of the unknown. Others have practiced yoga and meditation and been transported from the ordinary to the extraordinary in that way.

In esoteric astrology Neptune is said to govern devotion. Most people are devoted to something in their lives, often concrete matters like money, romantic partners, and personal creative pursuits. In addition, many people are attracted to a guru who teaches something different from what they learned as children. In this case, unfortunately, many individuals simply transfer their loyalty to the guru, without understanding the choices involved, and without coming to terms with the changes in boundaries. Neptune also signals just this sort of less conscious decision-making process.

With Neptune, the outcome of cyclical milestones often depends on the attitude of the individual. If the attitude is one of desire, then any benefits will come primarily through the material realm. Attitudes will include emotional responses and physical desire. If aspiration is the focus, then the results of Neptune transitions will include spiritual growth and development. In this case attitudes will have shifted toward a more spiritual expression of love and toward aspiration of the soul toward divine consciousness.

Alice Bailey stated that the "inner alignment and attitude" bring about "esoteric stimulation which awakens, in the disciple, the power of abstract thought."[20] While this statement is quite lofty, it relates directly to the transition we experience around the time of the first Neptune milestone at about age fourteen. It is at this time that most people gain the capacity for abstract thought. Before this time, most learning relates to concrete thinking and the development of deductive reasoning. Abstract thought goes a step further, integrating the capacity to consider things that can't be expressed through the ordinary senses, although we feel emotions associated with abstractions.

When material considerations and confused emotions prevent the advent of abstract thought, we find a case of arrested development. Such an individual continues into adulthood, still laboring under the belief that all matters are susceptible to personal manipulation and that life can somehow be completely predictable and controlled. It can take years to overcome this ingrained belief, and in fact, some people never get past this challenge. As we explore the Neptune cycle, we will see how spiritual life unfolds naturally, and we will also see how a refusal at the first milestone can cause a good deal of pain. We don't stop desiring to develop the spiritual, but we may stop being able to experience that growth.

It seems to me that a central theme relating to Neptune is the paradox. A paradox is a statement or situation that contains self-contradictory elements. Young children don't tolerate paradoxes well. They become frustrated, angry, and upset when situations can't be resolved. Usually parents or other adults step in to resolve the conflict, and children come to depend on adults for this. If the hurdle of abstract thought is not passed successfully, then paradoxical situations continue to provide irresolvable frustration and the individual has to resort to childlike reactions.

Here is another way to look at the paradox: When we consider a set of premises, and through deductive reasoning, arrive at two different results, we have encountered a paradox. We experience this sort of thing all the time with the people we know. For example, a parent can take us shopping for things we need, feed us healthy food, and tend our childhood injuries gently and lovingly. The same parent can have angry outbursts or even rages, accusing us of being dirty (a natural outcome of having fun), sneaky (a natural outcome of testing boundaries and independence) and incorrigible (only a very few people fit this definition). But here we are, very confused. We have this very good parent who loves us and this very bad parent who appears to hate us. This is a paradox. How can it be resolved?

The child often suppresses one side or the other because the conflict is intolerable. If we want to function well and happily as adults, we may have to go back to look at the parental situation again. We have to find a way to resolve the paradox. Without the capacity for abstract thought, we can't even hallucinate a way out of the problem. I have to say that I don't tolerate paradoxes very well, after all these years. I am better at identifying the two sides of the question, and then seeking a third possibility. The synthesis of elements from both sides of the paradox is generally needed to find the third possibility.

When you look in the dictionary for the word paradox, you will find, just above it, the word paradigm. A paradigm is a pattern, or a model of how things work. When you resolve a paradox, you produce a new mini-paradigm. In our example of the good parent-bad parent, one possible synthesis is no parent. We simply leave that person behind, never to be considered again. I don't know many (if any) people who have accomplished this. Another more creative possibility is to decide that this parent who loved me (I have concrete evidence of that) was not consistently loving (I remember instances of that). However, I can love this parent in spite of the inconsistencies. I no longer have to love everything my parent did (I can even continue to hate the destructive behavior), but I can love my parent as a human being. In the process I have learned that no human, even myself, can be perfectly consistent. The new mini-paradigm now states that people are not perfect. They can hold inconsistent beliefs and they can act inconsistently, and I can still be safe around them. The new paradigm provides a context for me to be happier.

One of the joys of spiritual development is that we all can hold beliefs on the spiritual level, and they will gradually manifest in our physical, emotional, and mental activities. On the spiritual level we can actively aspire to perfect possibilities, while accepting on every other level that we are aspiring—we are not there yet, and we don't have to be perfect all the time.

Now let's take a look at the Neptune milestones. Neptune is in a sign for about fourteen years. This means that each thirty-degree aspect to Neptune in the birth chart will occur on cycles of just under fourteen years, and this cycle is fairly regular. There can be as many as five passes to the exact position, depending on the timing of Neptune's retrogrades.

Neptune Aspects: Age, Aspect and Description

Semisextile, 13.7 years: Psychic ability may first emerge. Many teenagers have flashes of telekinesis, clairvoyance, and other extrasensory abilities.

Sextile, 27.5 years: There is an unfocused approach to life at this time. You are able to replace the familiar surroundings, acquaintances, and ideas with less familiar experiences. There is a potential for expansion into new psychological territory. This milestone sometimes coincides with the first Saturn return, or the first lunar return by progression, creating nuances that make this time period especially intense.

Square, 41.2 years: "The Neptune square to itself is probably the most critical aspect of its life cycle that we'll get to experience in our lifetime. It's associated with much of the growing disillusionment that we can feel with our current life pattern."[21] A time of inner conflict; growth of self-compassion; beginning of spiritual self-transcendence. "New inner foundation, based on values more universal than society has offered."

Trine, 54.9 years: Peak of spiritual expansion; opening to the non-material side of our existence. Transforming according to a more ideal but realistic self-image.[22]

Quincunx, 68.6 years: This and the later transit could signal health problems that are difficult to diagnose.

Opposition, 82 years: Resolution of false assumptions about the self; reversals of emotional attitude; self-illumination, if we begin to withdraw into our inner world in a state of serenity.[23]

Quincunx, 96.1 years: Another period when infections are possible, or diagnosis of health problems is difficult.

Trine, 109.9 years: Only a handful of individuals live to see this milestone.

Neptune in Action

Frequently the aspects of Neptune are followed or preceded by a Saturn aspect to the birth chart. William Butler Yeats provides a good example of this synchronizing of the two cycles.

Yeats' natal Neptune is in the second house in Aries. It is not part of the major grand trine and kite configurations in the chart, and we might think it is not as significant an indicator of Yeats' life and writing as the Sun-Jupiter opposition, for example. However, Neptune is within a two-degree orb of the quindecile (165 degree) aspect to Saturn, and Saturn in the eighth house is part of the kite pattern. Yeats' work is filled with symbols and ideas that speak to the most mystical side of Neptune. Ricki Reeves states about the quindecile of Saturn and Neptune, "Rigid structure may disappear. Idealism may dissolve old systems. Compassion may merge with authority. Dreams may become reality."[24] In other places, Ricki mentions the tendency to lose oneself in one's work.

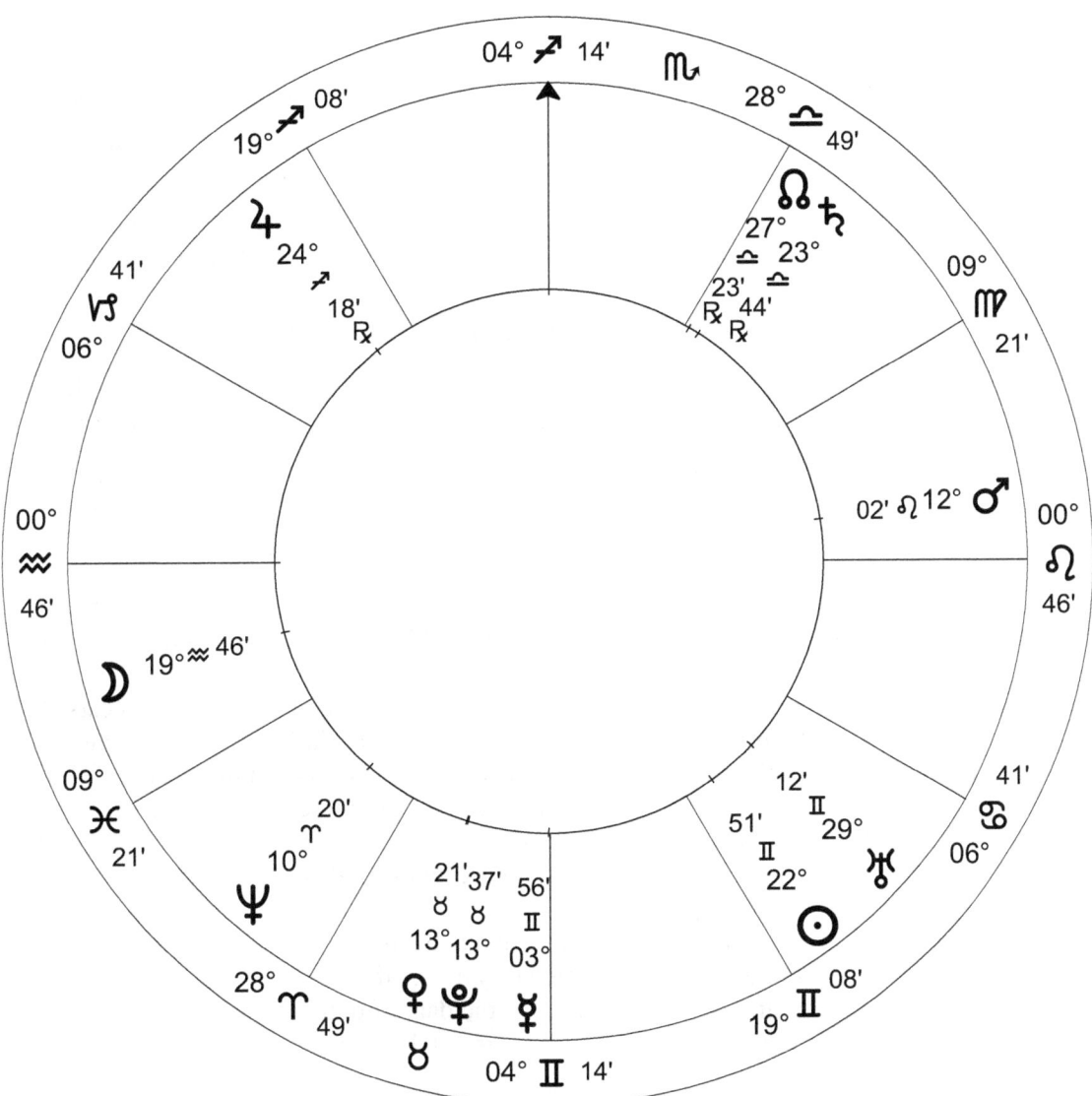

William Butler Yeats June 13, 1865, 10:40 pm, Dublin, Ireland
Tropical Koch

Illustration of Neptune and Saturn Aspects, William Butler Yeats

Natal Positions
Natal Neptune 10 Aries 21
Natal Saturn 23 Libra 45

Transiting Aspect	*Transit Date*	*Transit Positions*
Neptune semisquare natal Neptune	July 29, 1885	Neptune 25 Taurus 21
	September 28, 1885	Neptune 25 Taurus 21 retrograde
	May 17, 1886	Neptune 25 Taurus 21
	January 1, 1887	Neptune 25 Taurus 21 retrograde
	March 9, 1887	Neptune 25 Taurus 21
Saturn square natal Saturn	June 30, 1887	Saturn 23 Cancer 45
Saturn conjunction natal Saturn	October 22, 1923	Saturn 23 Libra 45
Neptune sesquisquare natal Neptune	September 9, 1926	Neptune 25 Leo 21
	February 24, 1927	Neptune 25 Leo 21 retrograde
	July 12, 1927	Neptune 25 Leo 21
Saturn semisquare natal Saturn	November 21, 1927	Saturn 08 Sagittarius 45

There were other examples of synchronous Saturn and Neptune phase aspects in Yeats' life. The two illustrated here occurred at particularly significant times in his life, and triggered the kite pattern and the quindecile between Saturn and Neptune. The first set of dates includes the time when he first met Madame Blavatsky and solidified his interest in esoteric matters. As Neptune moved from Taurus to Gemini in 1888, he joined the esoteric section of the Theosophical Society. His writings demonstrate the depth of his interest in theosophy and astrology.

The second set of dates center on the time he wrote and publish *A Vision*, his most esoteric work, in January 1926. This work includes a poem called "Phases of the Moon" and an extended explanation of what Yeats meant by these phases. On the date of publication, transiting Neptune was within one degree of the exact sesquisquare to its natal position.

Because the nature of Neptune is to dissolve boundaries, it is difficult to tie Neptune phases to precise events. Rather, the phases are characterized by a feeling or sense of possibilities. In Yeats' life, he may well have felt the Saturn return of October 22, 1923, much more sharply than he felt the upcoming Neptune phase. An example of the more obvious impact of Saturn is the fact that Yeats won a Nobel Prize in December 1923, just after his Saturn return. Additional awareness was no doubt provided at the time that Mars was square its natal position December 2, 1925, probably in the midst of preparing *A Vision* for printing.

Yeats, from his childhood, had a rich range of ideas concerning religion and spiritual subjects. He was familiar with myth and folklore of his native Ireland and drew upon those themes in much of his writing. His book *A Vision* baffles scholars to this day, as it stands outside the main body of his work and includes mystical and astrological references that are difficult to decipher.

Yeats exemplifies the nature of Neptune in many ways. With some friends, he founded the Dublin Hermetic Order in 1885. Yeats attended séances and was active in the Dublin Theosophical Lodge. He led the Hermetic Order of the Golden Dawn, starting in 1900. His wife devoted time each day to automatic writing, and those efforts are recorded in *A Vision*, along with Yeats' own formulation of a system of images.

Astrologers would expect the Neptune cycle to be important in Yeats' life, and they would not be disappointed. During the first milestone of transiting Neptune semisquare its position in Yeats' birth chart, a transit which lasted from July 1885 to March 1887, Yeats published his first poems and an essay about another poet's work. In addition, he attended at art school in Dublin during this time. In May 1887, Yeats first met Madame Blavatsky.

In 1920, Yeats made a lecture tour in the United States. This tour coincided with the Neptune trine, a transit that lasted for nearly a year. The Neptune sesquisquare period of 1926 to 1927 came after Yeats won the Nobel Prize in December 1923. This period saw the first version of *A Vision* published.

I must note that the Neptune milestones mentioned here are also associated with Saturn milestones. The first Neptune cycle ended less than four months before a Saturn square ; the second was interwoven with a triple Saturn transit to semisquare natal Saturn; and the third ended about four months before a Saturn semisquare. Around the time of this Saturn aspect, Yeats suffered from lung congestion and spent the winter in southern Spain.

Kurt Cobain

Kurt Cobain shares the kite configuration that we saw in Yeats' birth chart, suggesting the wealth of possibilities for both men. Cobain's Kite includes all the outer planets except Mars. With no squares involving planets, and no tight conjunctions, one might think this is a rather relaxed pattern. However, the oppositions tell a different story. With Uranus and Pluto bracketing the Ascendant, Cobain exemplified the concerns of his generation, and his band was highly successful for that reason. Cobain got his first guitar when Neptune formed the semisextile to its natal position. Within six years, he was on his way, forming Nirvana, his group, touring, and making records. Only ten years after he started, he smashed his first guitar when Saturn formed a square. The first Saturn square occurred during a period when his parents were already on their way to a divorce.

He left a suicide note in which he said, "I have felt guilty for so many years . . . the worst crime is faking it. I don't have any passion any more."[25]

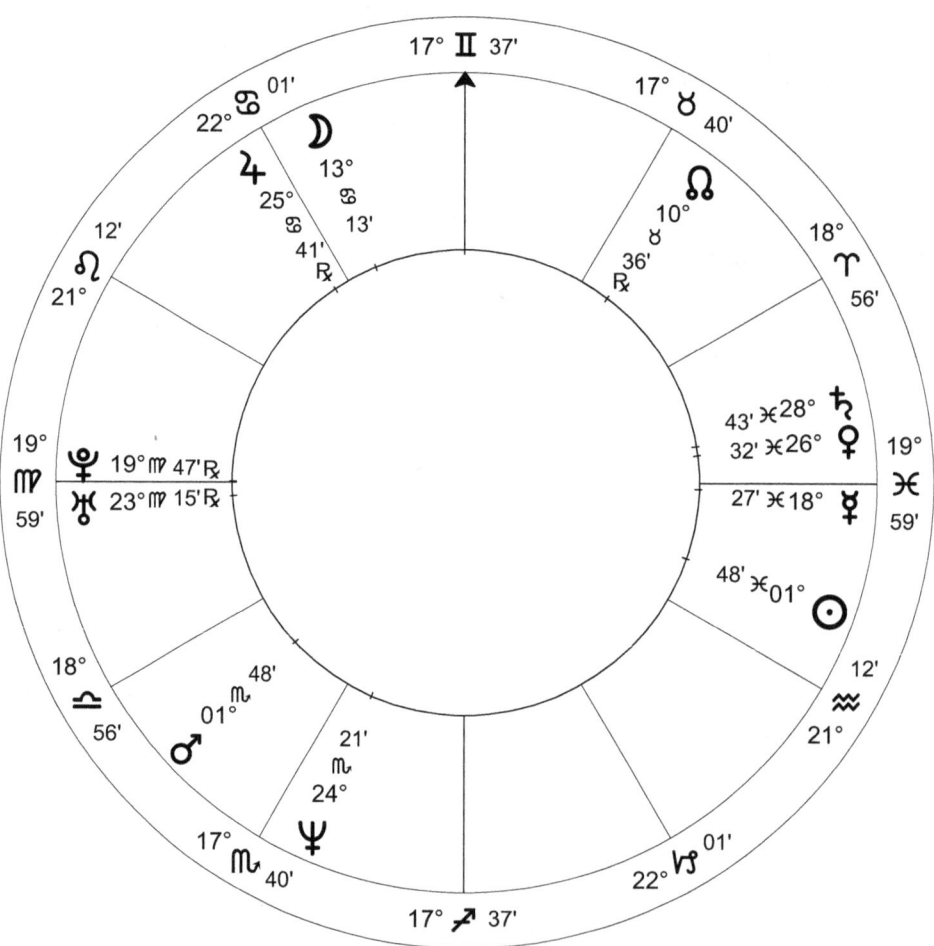

Kurt Cobain, February 20, 1967, 7:20 pm, Aberdeen, Washington
Tropical Koch

Neptune and Saturn

Because of the retrograde periods of the two planets, the interface of the Neptune and Saturn cycles relative to the birth chart can vary significantly. Neptune is in one sign about fourteen years, coinciding with half a Saturn cycle. When examining any chart, it is helpful to keep the relationship of the two planets in mind, as Saturn reflects the connections that can be made between the more spiritual, psychic, impressionable Neptune and the concrete, material side of life.

Elizabeth Taylor

Born with the Sun opposition Neptune with one degree of exact orb, Elizabeth Taylor has not had an easy life physically or emotionally. Reinhold Ebertin says that the Sun/Neptune connec-

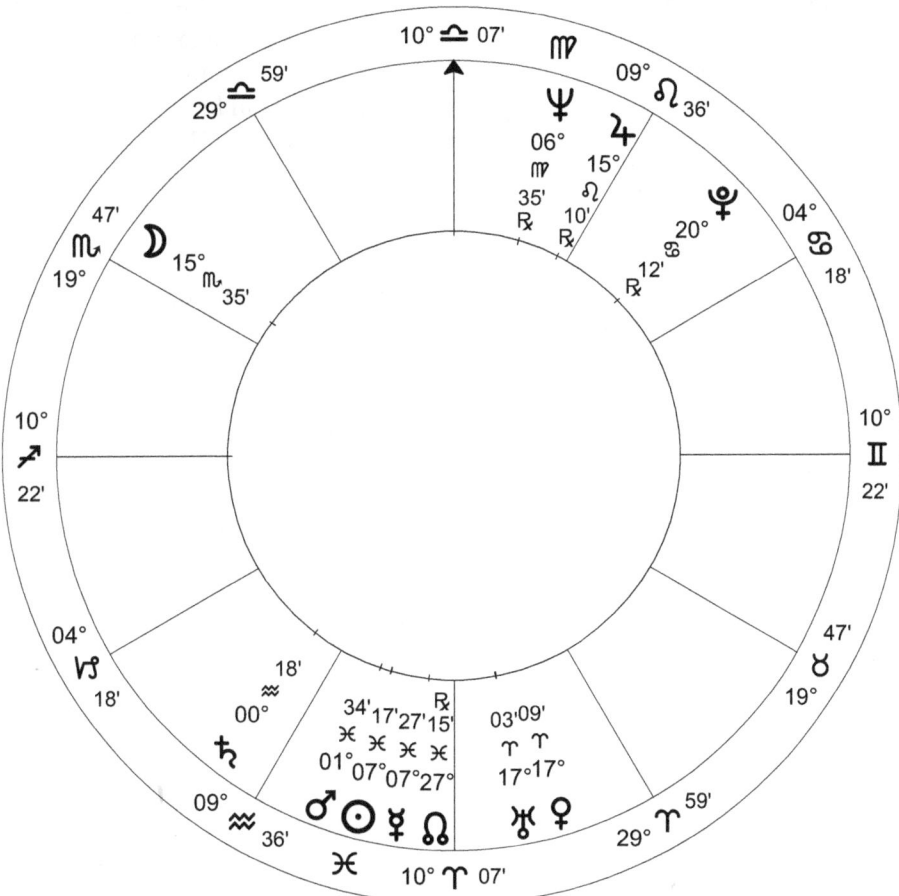

Elizabeth Taylor, February 27, 1932, 2:15 am, London, England
Tropical Koch

tion indicates "receptiveness to all impressions, an active imagination, and the faculty of enthusiasm," on the one hand, and "susceptibility, weakness, and self-deception" on the other. Physical indications include "sluggish cells, illness, disappointment, and proneness to seduction."[26]

We know through the media that Liz did her share of the seducing, and we also know she has had her share of very difficult illnesses, including two bouts with pneumonia, broken back (more than once), a benign brain tumor, skin cancer, and a diagnosis of congestive heart failure.

Looking at the list of transiting Neptune aspects, we see that in every case Neptune made either three or five passes over natal Neptune, each reflecting the fact that she was born with Neptune retrograde and had a rare Neptune conjunction at about five months of age. While such a series of multiple Neptune aspects to its natal position is not rare, I feel the close natal opposition to the Sun and Mercury, combined with the multiple transits, has accounted to some degree for her rise to stardom and her ability to intrigue audiences, even today. Her first Academy Award, for *Butterfield 8*, came after filming during the Neptune sextile, as did her first bout of pneumonia. *Who's Afraid of Virginia Wolf*, her second Academy Award, was filmed during her Neptune quintile.

Summary

The subtle qualities of Neptune are often hidden among the more obvious transits of other planets. In addition, most of us don't have the high drama that Elizabeth Taylor has experienced, nor the visionary experiences of W. B. Yeats.

The next chapter considers Pluto. If you thought the Neptune cycle was strange, brace yourself for a big surprise!

Chapter Ten

Pluto Cycle

Pluto's extremely eccentric orbit produces the most dramatic differences in timing of transits to its natal position. As we will see, normal lifetimes at some point in the cycle will include a Pluto square, while at other times individuals will easily live to see the Pluto opposition. In childhood, the differences are already dramatic. A child born when Pluto is moving quickly through the signs will have the first semisextile in the early teens, while during the slower end of the cycle a person will not have this surge of power until after age thirty. These are incredible differences. Of course, all of your peer group will have Pluto moving at the same speed, or very close to it, and the length of Pluto's cycle means that people born at the extremes will not be alive at the same time.

The differences are felt, however, in terms of generational influences. One's grandparents, for example, could have Pluto moving a good deal more slowly through their charts. The following information itemizes the transits of Pluto, including information about the age range during which each transit could occur. You will quickly see that certain adult developmental processes can occur much sooner for almost everyone alive on the planet today than they did for people born around 1800 to 1850, when Pluto was at its slowest. The differences are reflected in the dramatic shifts we are currently experiencing in every area of our lives, and the lack of relaxation in our lives.

Pluto Cycle Parallels

Because of the enormous variation in the timing of aspects in the Pluto cycle, I have included this table to show other planets' aspects to their natal position that may occur at about the same time as the Pluto aspects. The Pluto aspects are in italics.

Planet, Age, Aspect, and Developmental Process Or Issue

Retrograde/direct Pluto conjunction up to 272 days after birth: This aspect involves the will to live, the first cry, and the first breath.

Pluto semisextile, 12 to 31 years: The first awareness of psychic powers may develop, with the awareness that psychic powers are unusual or different from what other people perceive; there could be a capacity for telekinesis; awareness of personal power.

Saturn quincunx, 12.3 years: Third molars (wisdom teeth) may or may not appear.

Neptune semisextile, 13.7 years: Psychic ability may first emerge.

Uranus sextile, 14 years: Sexual and emotional opportunities arise; there is a desire to reach out to form strong relationships with others.

Saturn opposition, 14.7 years: Drastic movement from childhood to adulthood occurs here. The development of mental capabilities includes analytical thinking and critical evaluation of information. You are more capable of abstract thought. Sexuality becomes an issue between you and your parents. There may be rebellion, and the evading of responsibility for your actions. You test the limits of behavior. You may move beyond your peer group attachments, as you no longer depend on their approval as much.

Saturn trine, 19.6 years: This aspect coincides approximately with the completion of the first Metonic cycle of eclipses. There may be a period of relaxation during which emotional energy can be accommodated by the personality in new ways. Memory capacity may grow or change.

Uranus square, 21 years: There is a mental crisis. Your sense of the future—your intuition—strives to see what is ahead, and you learn new ways of planning for the future.

Saturn square, 22.2 years: Now there is a "crisis of consciousness." You are ending the period of dependence upon your parents. You can stand alone. You have mental individuality (yet you are not a hermit). There are many philosophical questions arising for you. You may have your first adult romantic relationship—that is, the first romantic relationship that is not based on some form of dependency.

Pluto sextile, 24 to 61 years: "An underground force helping to rid us of non-essentials in our life. It can clear the way for new starts, like a gentle sweep of a big broom rather than a bulldozer mowing down whatever's in its path. We feel encouraged to let go of part of our past that have short-changed our potential."[27]

Saturn sextile, 24.1 years: This aspect approximately coincides with the second Jupiter return. Intellectual capacity aligns with the awareness of structure in one's life. Career and business concerns are a focus.

Saturn semisextile, 27 years: For some people, this aspect coincides with first lunar return by progression. Maturing emotions meet with painful realizations about how life has progressed to this point. Sort of an "early" Saturn return.

Neptune sextile, 27.5 years: There is an unfocused approach to life at this time. You are able to replace the familiar surroundings, acquaintances, and ideas with less familiar experiences. There is a potential for expansion into new psychological territory.

Uranus trine, 28 years: You become more conscious of your own ego and how it functions. There is greater intuitive development at this time.

Saturn conjunction, 29.5 years: There is a shift from the growth period into the productive cycle represented by Saturn's second transit through your chart.

Uranus quincunx, 35 years: A psychological or emotional crisis may occur, with intuitive awareness suggesting solutions that would have been rejected earlier. The capacity to make adjustments that are personally beneficial develops.

Neptune square, 41.2 years: "The Neptune square to itself is probably the most critical aspect of its life cycle that we'll get to experience in our lifetime. It's associated with much of the growing disillusionment that we can feel with our current life pattern." This is a time of inner conflict; growth of self-compassion; beginning of spiritual self-transcendence. "New inner foundation, based on values more universal than society has offered."[28]

Uranus opposition, 42 years: Psychological reorganization occurs. You find some success on the social level. The psychological upheaval relates to intimate relationship in the romantic, social, and/or professional spheres. This can be a confusing time, as you are changing your thinking on fundamental issues.

Uranus quincunx, 49 years: Changes in religious or spiritual affiliations occur, or there is a deepening of spiritual beliefs. A better understanding of transcendent values.

Neptune trine, 54.9 years: There is a peak of spiritual expansion, opening to the non-material side of our existence. Transformation occurs according to a more ideal but realistic self-image.[29]

Uranus trine, 56 years: You may have a resurgence (or beginning) of occult experiences. There is a sexual upheaval. For women this is the likely timing of menopause, although you may have felt it approaching for some time. For men it may be a time of re-thinking your sexual activities. There is emotional conflict associated with these sexual changes. You may be seeking to reclaim your youth in some way.

***Pluto square, 36 to 86 years:** Depending on the date of birth, the potential age range for the occurrence of this aspect is vast. Considering the power of this phase angle of Pluto to the natal position, the difference in age can make a huge difference in the developmental path of the individual, and for the generations in which early or late transits occur. "Many structures in our current life have outgrown their purpose and are ready to be broken down and swept away. We need to make sure that we don't get swept away with them."*[30]

Uranus square, 63 years: There is a theoretical chance for a third birth, associated with the second Saturn return and the Uranus square. You harvest the fruits of your past efforts. You are born into wisdom if your intuitive development has proceeded well. You now are able to teach what you have learned.

Neptune quincunx, 68.6 years: Adjustments in your way of thinking concern the house and sign where Neptune is found. Adapting to the mentor role and its demands takes place.

Uranus sextile, 70 years: This is a period of extensive abstract thought and social fulfillment. You gain greater wisdom during this period.

Uranus semisextile, 77 years: This is a time to integrate concepts of change and structure in new ways. There could be changes in bodily rhythms, and also a release of physical and emotional tension.

***Pluto trine, 52 to 115 years:** Sensitivity to a larger world view "that instill within us a sense of hope for deeper human understanding and global unity. Technology may excite us as never be-*

fore . . . heightened self-awareness as we happily tap into latent inner resources . . . easier to shed old, outgrown roles . . . open doors to spiritual perception."[31]

Neptune opposition, 82.4 years: Resolution of false assumptions about the self; reversals of emotional attitude; self-illumination, if we begin to withdraw into our inner world in a state of serenity.[32]

Uranus conjunction, 84 years: There is a "symbolic climax for our soul's development. We have officially completed our assignment on Earth regarding our mundane 'contract' with society and the roles we felt somewhat roped into playing . . . challenge lies in how we embark on our inner journey in consciousness."[33]

Neptune quincunx, 96.1 years: More people are reaching this point in the Neptune cycle. This can be a critical period physically, as susceptibility to viruses and infection is greater. It can also be a very peaceful period in which psychic connections are strengthened.

Pluto quincunx, 65 to 140 years: *A period of adjustment to shifts within the psyche, and in the physical body. Ideas about your life path may be revitalized as you seek new ways to engage the world.*

Neptune trine, 109.9 years: Only a handful of individuals live to see this milestone.

Pluto opposition, 85 to 160 years: *"People born in the fall of 1937 . . . will have this transiting opposition no earlier than early spring of 2023 at the age of eighty-six . . . fuller perspective . . . deeply evaluate the societal framework in which we were born . . . burn off any residual negativity that would only weigh our soul down. We probably need to forgive."*[34]

While the above listing suggests pinpointed milestones for Pluto's transit, we actually feel the onset of the aspect for months or years in advance. The effect is rather like the sound and vibration of a freight train coming. You can hear or feel it long before it is in sight, and long after it has passed. Pluto's impact is felt beforehand in terms of pressure building. We feel conflicts associated with our own use of power and will well before we are forced to make many decisions, and we feel the impact of those decisions long after the exact aspect has passed.

Modern psychology provides us with a model of the psyche and reveals that there are vast depths to be explored. Even though Kore was unhappy to find herself in the underworld, there were doubtless some interesting features to attract her attention. Many people never want or need to examine their psychological depths. Those who do discover connections to their hidden, dark side, to spiritual values and resources, and to stories and metaphors that enrich their lives. It is often through the auspices of Pluto that we discover our personal myths and understand how they play our in our lives. It is through Pluto that we understand many facets of our vocational or spiritual missions.

Early Pluto Square, Mid-1900s

Two gymnasts and a Supreme Court Chief Justice provide excellent examples of lives in which Pluto transits to square its birth position very early on. in life. While their careers are very different, there are parallels that reflect the "speedy" quality experienced by an entire generation. Olga Korbut was born on May 16, 1955, and Nadia Comaneci was born November 12, 1961. John Roberts was born on January 27, 1955. All three of these individuals rose to prominence in their fields early in life.

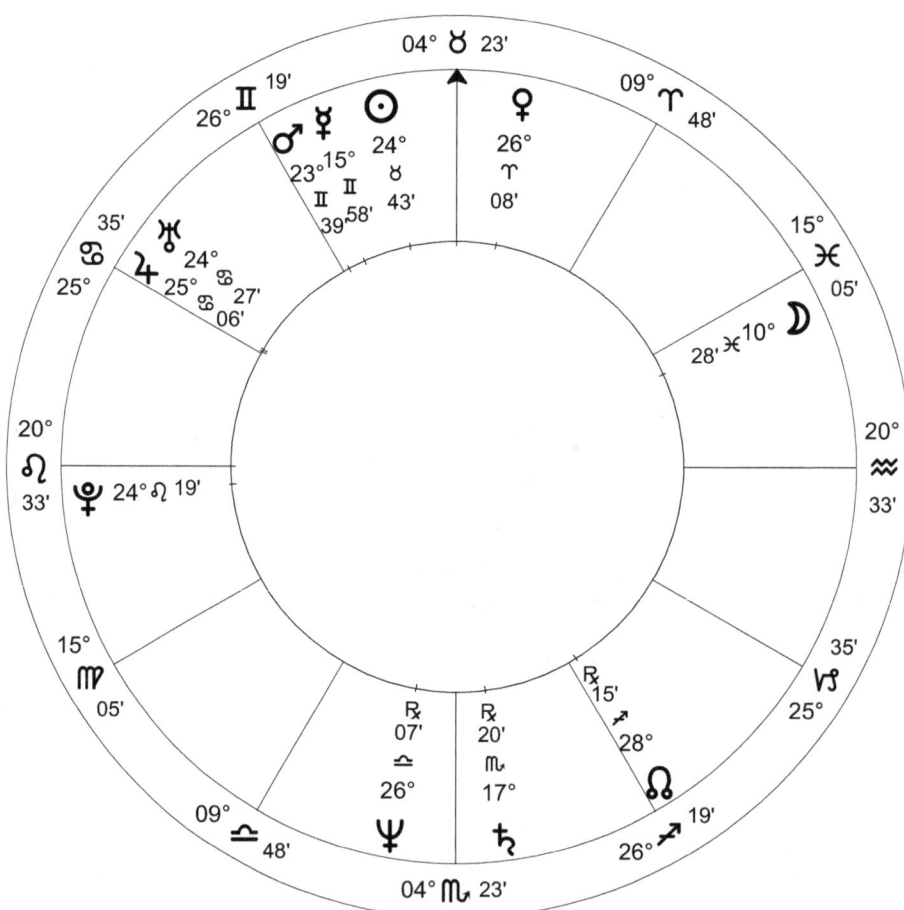

Olga Korbut, May 16, 1955, 12:00 pm, Grodno, Belarus
Tropical Koch

It's a toss up to decide which female gymnast contributed more to the sport, Olga Korbut or Nadia Comaneci. While Olga Korbut was earning her second set of gold and silver medals in Olympic gymnastics and Nadia earned her first three gold medals, John Roberts was studying law and graduating *summa cum laude* from Harvard in three years. He was the managing editor of the *Harvard Law Review* in 1978-1979, possibly as impressive an honor as *summa cum laude*.

What makes these three such vivid examples of the early Pluto square is that they all achieved prominence very early in their lives. Because of this they exemplify the quality of the early Pluto square, which tends to drive many individuals to accomplish as much as possible as quickly as possible.

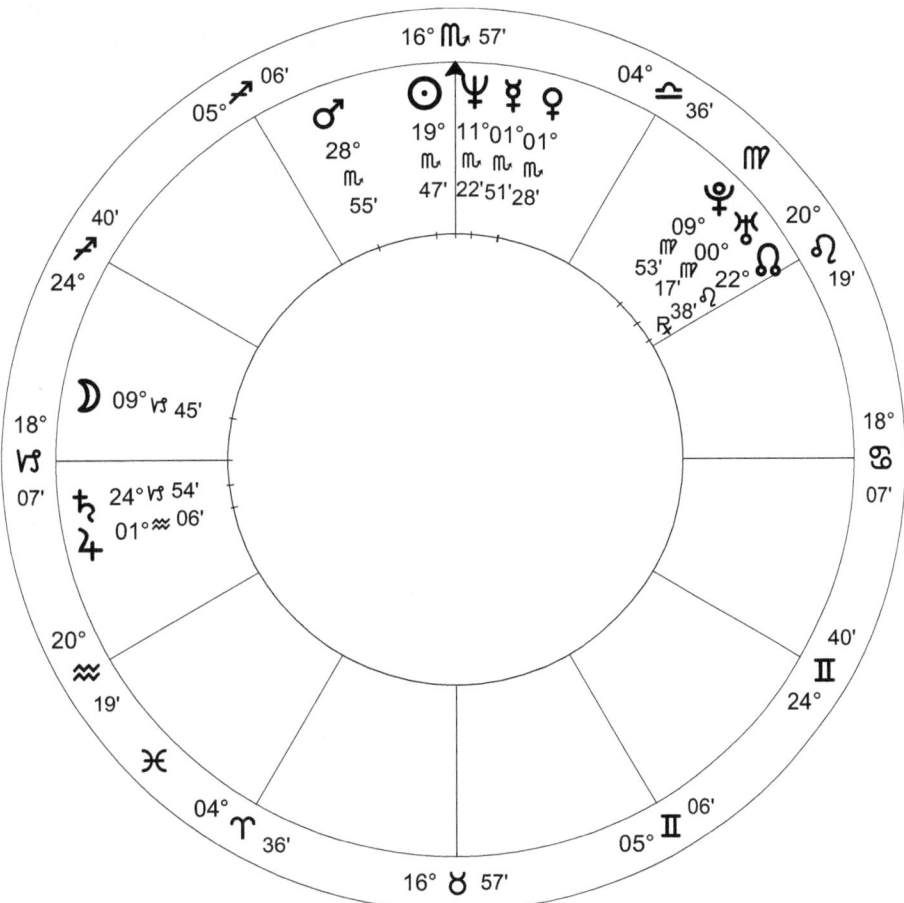

Nadia Comaneci, November 12, 1961, 12:00 pm, Orastie, Romania
Troical Koch

The three also reveal the positive and the not so constructive effects of the quick rise to power and prominence that is reflected in Pluto's transit. Nadia won her first Olympic medals when she was just fourteen (after her first Saturn opposition in August 1975). In 1980, she was approaching the Pluto semisquare which lasted from November 1981 to August 1982. It was during this period that she retired from competition. Her defection to the United States came only months before her first Saturn return. She promoted gymnastic apparel and other products for several years. In 1996, she married American gymnast Bart Conner. They have a gymnastic academy, a production company, and several other businesses. By age forty-five she was already well into her third career and looking forward to becoming a mother.

Olga Korbut didn't have such smooth sailing. She appeared to be the quintessential gymnast, performing tricks that no one seems able to duplicate. She competed at the Olympics in 1972 and 1976, and wowed everyone, including the judges. She breathed life into the sport of women's gymnastics in the United States.

When she retired from competition, she completed a college degree and coached the Belarus gymnastics team. She immigrated to the U.S. in 1991 with her family. According to wikipedia.org,[35] she was caught shoplifting, and her son was caught with counterfeit currency. She is divorced and remarried. According to PBS,[36] Olga Korbut "accused her former coach of having made her his sex slave and the Soviet National Olypmic Committee of having confiscated her gold medals from her." Her star quality is not tarnished by these allegations, but they serve as indicators that being in the spotlight has its down side, especially for people as young as she was at the time. In this she is rather like many people in her generation who have struggled to find jobs that they enjoy and relationships that last.

Granted that John Roberts was not appointed to the Supreme Court until age fifty, he is still among the youngest to become chief justice. Only John Jay, the first chief justice, and John Marhsall were younger when they became chief more than 200 years earlier.

Lest we fall into the trap of thinking that gymnasts necessarily succeed or fail in their careers much earlier than other people, note that John Roberts entered Harvard as a sophomore at age eighteen, and graduated *summa cum laude* in 1976, the year transiting Pluto made a semisquare to its position in his birth chart. Born the same year as Olga Korbut, he achieved dramatic academic success at the same time she was achieving athletic success. At the time he experienced the Pluto square, he had returned to private law practice after his nomination by George H. W. Bush to the U.S. Court of Appeals expired at the end of Bush's term as president. He finally did become a circuit court judge when George W. Bush nominated him in 2003, and became chief justice of the Supreme Court in 2005.

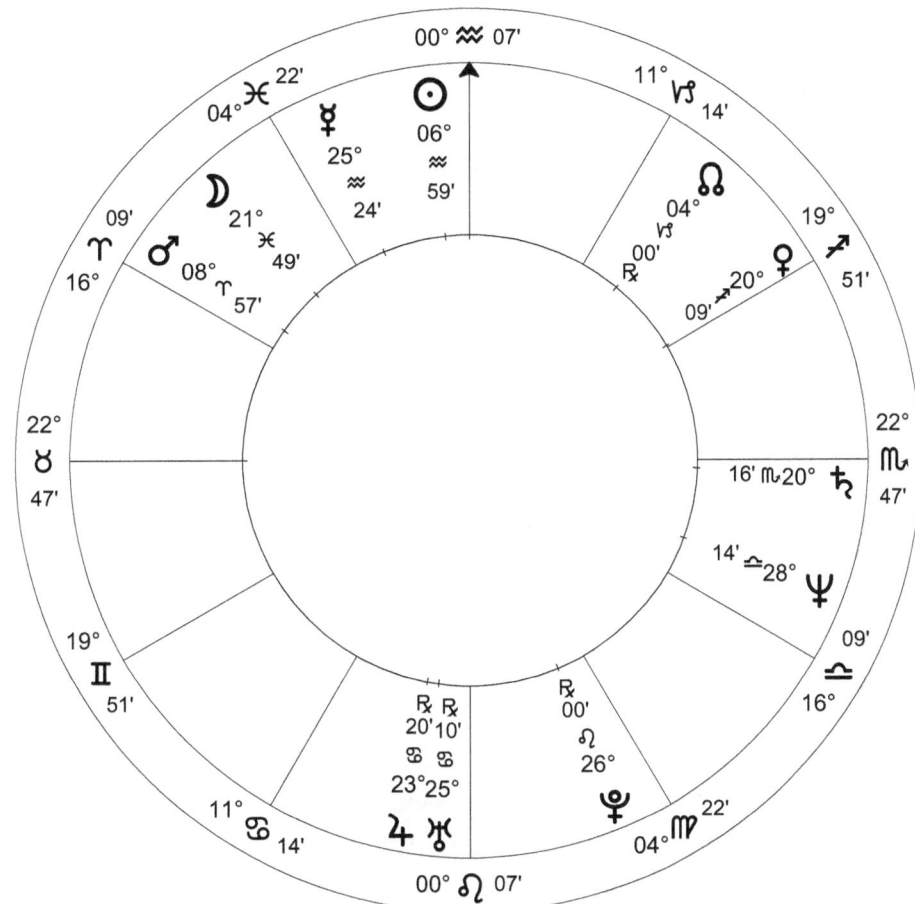

John Roberts, January 27, 1955, 12:00 pm, Buffalo, New York
Tropical Koch

Benjamin Franklin

Benjamin Franklin also experienced the Pluto square early in his life, along with many of the figures who were prominent in the period preceding and during the American Revolution. Although we don't have exact birth information for him, we don't really need it for the purpose of looking at the Pluto square, which occurred for him in 1744 and 1745, at the same time as the Neptune square, and before the Uranus opposition in 1746 and the Saturn opposition in 1748. By this point in his life Franklin had already run away from an apprenticeship position with his brother in a printing company, secretly written a column for that paper, traveled to England and worked there, worked for a Philadelphia merchant, set up his own printing business, achieved the status of grand master in the local Freemason lodge, sired at least one illegitimate son, entered into a common law marriage, and more.

In 1733, at age twenty-seven, he began publishing *Poor Richard's Almanac*, selling about 10,000 copies a year. Among his many inventions are the lightning rod, the Franklin stove, and bifocal glasses. In 1748, at the (early) age of forty-two, he retired from the printing business and took up other interests. His work with electricity led to the naming of units of electrical charge after him. He made discoveries about weather and refrigeration. He was also a musician.

Of course Ben Franklin is known as a political figure. He began in local politics, eventually reformed the postal system for the colonies, and served as a diplomat to Britain and France. His involvement in colonial politics led to the end of his career as deputy postmaster for North America, and he returned to Philadelphia in 1775. After that he helped to write the Declaration of Independence, spent time in France, eventually became an abolitionist, and freed his slaves. In this he stands in contrast to other founding fathers who retained their slaves in spite of what they espoused in the Declaration of Independence, Constitution, and Bill of Rights.

Note that Franklin was relatively long-lived for his time. Still, he had made a name for himself at a very early age, and continued to add to his résumé throughout his life.

Slow Pluto
Charles Darwin and Abraham Lincoln, born within hours of each other, serve as examples of a slow Pluto transit. Others, born about 260 years before, include Elizabeth I of England, John Dee, Ivan the Terrible, and Galileo. All of these individuals had long careers, and in many ways did not fulfill their promise until much later in life. Darwin traveled and studied, but delayed the publication of his life's work for many years due to the religious climate of the times. Lincoln wrote the Gettysburg Address a few years after his Pluto semisquare at age fifty-four. Contrast this with Olga Korbut and Nadia Comaneci, who had earned multiple gold medals by age twenty (after their Pluto semisquare).

The Point of All This
The point of all this biographical review is to reveal the relative speed people go through life. Note that during revolutionary periods of history, we have people experiencing the Pluto aspects very early in life. During slower periods, we have long-lived governments led by long-lived rulers and we see extended thought processes that take time to come to fruition.

If we take these cycles seriously, we will notice that young people born in the twenty-first century may seem more thoughtful than we did in our youth. They will not feel the Plutonian urge to push ahead as fast, and they may be the ones who take the time to discover ways to save the

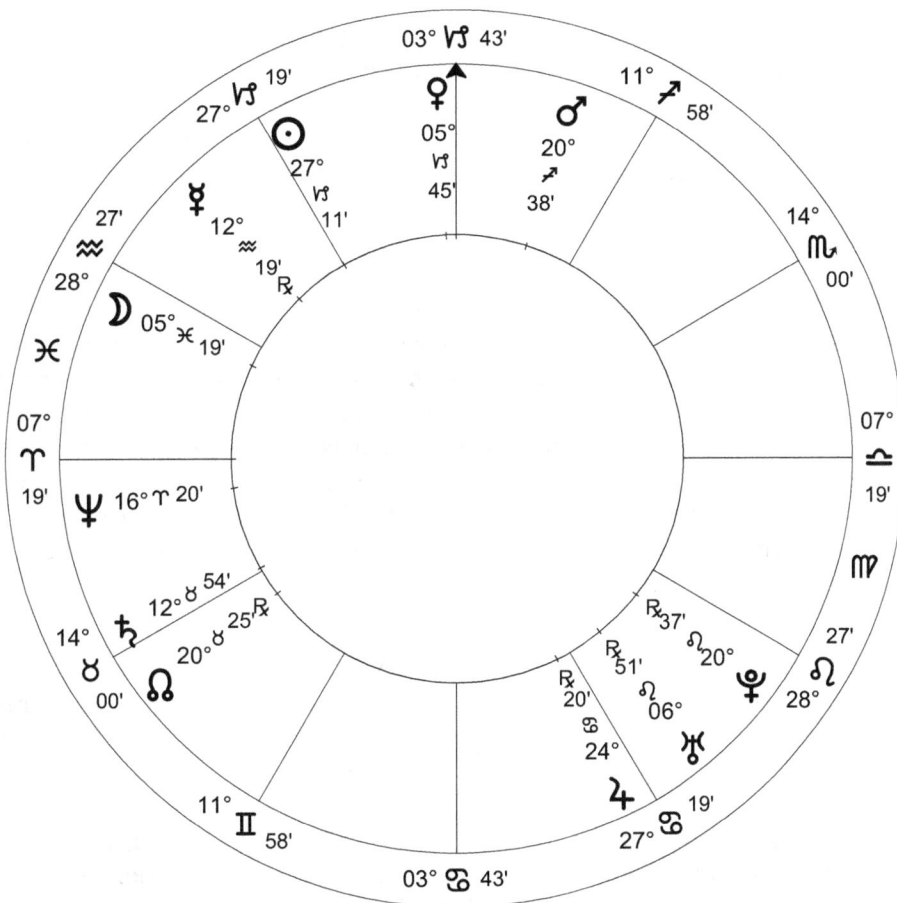

Benjamin Franklin, January 17, 1706, 10:30 am, Boston, Massachusetts
Tropical Koch

planet from the ravages of industrial and nuclear pollution. Wordsworth (born in 1770 and experiencing the Pluto square at age sixty-eight to seventy) captured the sense of needing to slow down in these lines:

> "The world is too much with us; late and soon,
> Getting and spending, we lay waste our powers."

These lines suggest a desire to proceed through life with greater decorum, enjoying life and taking thought for tomorrow as well. Born in 1770, and writing the above in 1804, at the time Pluto was moving slowest, Wordsworth suggests the possibility of greater power in moving more slowly.

Those of us who lived through the early Pluto square, experiencing it before the Uranus opposition, often felt our lives were out of synch in some ways. We may even have felt that we were backing into some of life's experiences. If people are at a maximum point of power before developing their intuitive capacity, for example, they may be less able to foresee the consequences of their actions. They are much more aware of how it feels to be powerful, and how it feels to exert force in their lives. They may be relatively unprepared for the moments when no amount of force will make things work properly for them.

By understanding the overlapping cycles of Uranus, Neptune, and Pluto, and the extreme variations in Pluto's cycle, we can help ourselves and our clients to understand what is happening in our lives. The differences are comparable, although on a different time scale, to the early or late occurrence of Venus aspects in infancy, and by extension, in secondary progressions. Venus, reflecting social development, revealed the possibility of accelerated or delayed social skills in relation to action and assertion (the Mars cycle). Pluto transits reflect a relative application of power to whatever we attempt. Darwin, by waiting for what must have seemed like a lifetime to publish his work, achieved a more lasting place in the literature of science than he may have if his theories were published in the face of extreme religious opposition.

Conclusion

I concluded long ago that astrology is meaningful in my life, and in the lives of my family, friends, and clients. Seeing the cycles of the planets unfold in people's lives, I continue to feel awe when confronted with the pattern laid down for us in the Universe.

The research for this book took me deeper into the nature of cycles. Even as I was finishing the writing, I was still discovering new concepts regarding how astrology works. The word conclusion is therefore the wrong choice for this last bit of information. I anticipate that I will continue to learn as I study astrology.

So far I have found that the first return cycle of each planet provides a map of human development in terms of physical, mental, emotional, and spiritual growth. The details of this truth should amaze you—every key developmental process can be linked to the cycles of one planet or another, or possibly the cycles of two or more planets. When I began, I did not anticipate the totality of what I found.

The astrological outlines in this book provide a précis of your life as it is reflected in astrology. It shows you how we all develop within the rhythm of variations in the particular planetary return cycles we experience. Your own chart provides information about the unique way you fulfill the human promise. If everyone had these two tools, they could track their lives, decide if they are going where they want to, and redirect their energies in ways that are appropriate with the model of our solar system within the sphere of the fixed stars.

Here are just a few of the implications of this study of planetary cycles. Understanding planetary cycles can:

Help parents to

- Know developmental issues that typically arise and when.
- Know how to manage or compensate for problems before they occur.

Help children to

- Understand change in their bodies, minds, and emotions.
- Know what to anticipate as they move into new phases of development.
- Manage out-of-control teenage emotions more effectively.
- Help children to understand the differences in their peers.

Help Adults to

- Understand what adult developmental issues may arise.
- Know ahead of time so that planning can happen.
- Know what to do about the issues.
- Put a creative plan into action.
- Potential impact on partnerships and what to do about that.

Help health care providers, teachers, and social service workers to

- Gauge the developmental progress of adults or children.
- Evaluate problems against a standard.
- Understand the variables within the standard.
- Develop plans to help people with delayed development.
- Know when to boost precocious development.

This book makes three essential points:

- There are so-called normal stages of human development, as defined by physicians and developmental psychologists.
- There are cycles of Sun, Moon, and planets throughout our solar system, as defined by astronomers and astrologers.
- These stages and cycles happen to line up very nicely and precisely, so that astrology describes every facet of human development.

Where do we go from here? The astrological model is as flexible as our minds. I hope that researchers one day will accept the parallels between the astrological model and the human development model, and use these tools together to help us live longer, better, and happier.

Appendix One
Planetary Cycles

This table gathers the aspects of each planet for the first return cycle. There is a bold heading before the first aspect for each planet, along with a few key words regarding development. The reader will note time spans given, particularly for Venus, Mars, and Pluto. These are necessary because of the retrograde timing in the case of Venus, and because of the eccentric orbit in the case of Pluto.

For all you parents out there, please note that the dates mentioned in this table represent average timing for developmental tasks. We know that the astrological markers associated with many developmental tasks vary in remarkable ways. We also know that infants are miracles of growth and development, and that in almost every case they meet the challenges and succeed at every stage of development.

The point of this table is to demonstrate that the meanings associated with astrological cycles parallel physical, emotional and mental developmental timetables very closely, thereby proving the theoretical basis of astrology.

Planet	**Age**	**Developmental Process or Issue**
Retrograde Mercury conjunct	Up to 48 days	Crisis of breathing, motor nervous system
Retrograde Venus conjunct	Up to 74 days	Crisis of organ function (kidneys)
Retrograde Mars conjunct	Up to 142 days	Crisis of fever or inflammation, red blood cells
Retrograde Jupiter conjunct	Up to 213 days	Crisis of assimilation of nutrients, weight gain (liver)
Retrograde Saturn conjunct	Up to 234 days	Crisis of structure, metabolic disorder, accumulation of toxins; ear problems
Retrograde Uranus conjunct	Up to 261 days	Crisis of accidental nature; rhythmic functions
Retrograde Neptune conjunct	Up to 272 days	Crisis of infection, paralysis, hidden problem; hypersensitive or abnormal organs or bodily functions
Retrograde Pluto conjunct	Up to 272 days	Crisis of regeneration, elimination, surgical intervention

Moon: Life and Nourishment on the Physical Plane

Moon semisextile	2.25 days	Consumption of nourishment should be in place. Breast milk comes in. Mother's body begins to adjust to the infant's feeding schedule and demand.
Moon sextile	4.5 days	Infant settles into basic eating, sleeping, diapering pattern.
Moon square	6.8 days	If nursing ability is not developed, a crisis develops at the age of one week. The baby needs nourishment to thrive. Weight gain needs to occur by this point in order to insure survival. This is the first challenging aspect of a planet to its own position to occur in an infant's life, and the challenge must be met. When the eating challenge is met at this first point of balance, the baby is on the road to successful growth and development.
Moon trine	9.1 days	Parents and infant may relax a bit as they become more familiar with each other and the new rhythms of daily life.
Moon quincunx	11.37 days	Parents may experience a day or two of resistance from the infant in the form of crying for no apparent reason, or restless sleep.
Moon opposition	13.7 days	The baby settles into a routine. By this time there may be more regular hunger patterns, although a pattern may not emerge this early. The parents will have become more familiar with the baby's needs, and will exert their influence to establish an orderly cycle to some extent.
Moon quincunx	15.92 days	Possible hiccup in what is otherwise seen as forward progress.
Moon trine	18.2 days	Settling into routine a bit more. Sleep patterns may stabilize, with more sleep at night for longer stretches of time.
Moon square	21 days	The challenge of nourishment has been met, weight gain is essential, getting stronger, movement of limbs is more organized.
Moon sextile	23 days	First smiles or other evidence of response from infant to parents' speech and touch.

Venus: Love, Capacity to Relate to Others; Organ Function

Venus semisextile	24/34 days	First social connections; the infant smiles and pats the mother while nursing.
Moon semisextile	25 days	Some apparently intentional movement.
Moon conjunct	27 days	Turns head sideways, moves limbs in large jerky motion (arms more than legs), begins to support head when pulled up; reflexive walking movements.

Mercury: Mind/Body Connection, Nervous System, Breath

Mercury semisextile	30 days	Infant makes sounds in response to speech. Parents can distinguish tone of crying.

Sun: Sustainer of Life, Giver of Heat and Energy; Will

Sun semisextile	30 days	Infant raises chest and turns head; head flops down toward back.
Venus sextile	49/68 days	Infant gazes at mother's face. This is the first sign of social competence. By four months, this tendency decreases.

Mars: Energy; Desire; Competition

Mars semisextile	57/65 days	Baby raises chest and turns head
Mercury sextile	60 days	The walking reflex may begin to disappear; grasping reflex also declines. This is a time when language capacity develops (using right hemisphere of brain).
Sun sextile	61 days	
Venus square	73/102 days	May snuggle more comfortably when held.
Mercury square	90 days	The baby brings hands together, reaches for objects but usually misses
Sun square	91 days	Laugh out loud, pay attention to objects, follow object past midline, smile spontaneously
Venus trine	97/136 days	
Mars sextile	114/129 days	Purposefully rolls over, from stomach to back; holds had erect and steady; may start to grasp objects; raises head and chest and stretches out arms; raises head and turns from side to side easily.

Mercury trine	119 days	Can look at and hold rattle at the same time
Venus quincunx	122/170 days	
Sun trine	122 days	The back is much straighter; baby sits with support
Venus opposition	145/204 days	Squeals, smiles, vocalizes and may say baby talk words, wave blow kiss, learn mama and dada
Mercury quincunx	149 days	The baby may start to grasp objects
Sun quincunx	152 days	
Venus quincunx	170/238 days	
Mars square	171/196 days	Will bear some weight on legs, sit without support, work to get a toy out of reach, will cry or object when toy is taken away.
Mercury opposition	179 days	Babble, turn in direction of a voice, grasp or pick up small object, say mama or dada indiscriminately, begins to learn concepts, "hear the cry," "soft bear!"
Sun opposition	183 days	Feed self a cracker, somewhat demanding, will object when a desire is not accommodated, begins to socialize, wave, laugh. Learns names, Mommy, Daddy, own name
Venus trine	194/272 days	
Mercury quincunx	209 days	
Sun quincunx	213 days	
Venus square	218/306 days	Play ball or other simple game, fear of strangers may occur
Mars trine	229/258 days	Play ball or other simple game, fear of strangers may occur
Mercury trine	239 days	
Venus sextile	242/340 days	Color conscious
Sun trine	244 days	
Venus semisextile	267/374 days	
Mercury square	269 days	Walk holding furniture, say Mama, may lay patty cake. Will use a method other than crying to communicate wants. Holding the breath.

Sun square	274 days	Looks for a dropped object, plays peek-a-boo, responds to simple directions, attachment to toys and other objects
Mars quincunx	286/401 days	
Venus conjunct	291/408 days	Alternately independent and clingy, can mimic actions, scribble/draw, enjoys picture books.
Mercury sextile	298 days	
Sun sextile	304 days	
Mercury semisextile	328 days	
Sun semisextile	335 days	
Mars opposition	343/394 days	Walk holding on, may walk well, drink from a cup, play ball
Mercury conjunct	358 days	May indicate wants without crying, says several words, may say a short sentence with baby talk words
		Age 2: More confident in speech, shows left or right handedness
Sun conjunct	365 days	Separation anxiety, may have favorite clothes.
		Age 2: Explores on one's own, more confidence; definite favorite clothes

Jupiter-Preserver; Higher Mind; Expansion into Environment; Confidence

Jupiter semisextile	1 year	Experience of successes in many activities that have required substantial effort to learn
Mars quincunx	1.1 to 1.3 years	Possibly encountering limits through painful experiences, such as injuries
Mars trine	1.3 to 1.4 years	Possibly accepting guidance from caretakers more readily
Mars square	1.4 to 1.6 years	May need to discourage biting and hitting. Some skills seem to be forgotten. Appetite varies. Behavior is unpredictable. Child uses the word "no" for everything.
Mars sextile	1.6 to 1.8 years	Increasing mobility; can walk, run.
Mars semisextile	1.7 to 2 years	Possibly entering the "terrible twos" when the child becomes very demanding.
Mars conjunct	1.9 to 2.2 years	Can place shapes on a matching board.

Jupiter sextile	2 years	The emphasis is on new relationships and the development of communication skills. The key is the power of communication in one's environment.
		Second cycle twelve years later involves the development of a new social outlook. Third cycle twenty-four years later involves the development of a new psychological outlook.

Saturn-Structure (Hair, Bones, Teeth); Experience; Karma/Dharma

Saturn semisextile	2.5 years	Second molars
Jupiter square	3 years	Here there is a crisis of choice. You choose the way to go, and then work within the limits of that path. There is a concentration of intention. The focus is on action; social skills learned here carry through all the cycles.
Jupiter trine	4 years	Going forward with the skills that have been learned, there is some degree of risk-taking. You demonstrate some of the values you have absorbed. There is a need to gain self assurance at this stage. Asks "why."
Saturn sextile	4.9 years	Opportunities to learn new information, gain new responsibilities, and develop a daily rhythm or schedule.
Jupiter quincunx	5 years	There are adjustments to increasing social activities and introduction to formal schooling.
Jupiter opposition	5.9 years	With the end of the first half of the Jupiter cycle, there is an effort to perfect relationships. You show your ability to adapt to social situations. There are more expansive feelings and greater self confidence. Three is a sense of personal power. Has an ideal self ("I want to be..."). Can answer a "what if" question. Boys generally about six months behind girls in development. Can recognize some strange faces. Can climb, dance. Can describe the self in physical terms.
Jupiter quincunx	6.9 years	More adjustments can be expected with this aspect, with a growing understanding of right and wrong that goes beyond simple awareness of consequences. The associated Uranus and Saturn aspects may blend to cause the as-

trologer confusion about which planet is related to which developmental factor.

Uranus-Intuition; Individualized Action; Disruption; Equilibrium

Uranus semisextile	6 to 7 years	Understands ambiguity; understands words with two meanings; understands words that sound alike. Understands sarcasm. Can describe personal feelings
Saturn square	7.4 years	There is an attempt to emphasize the "I" in the personality. The child questions authority of parents and teachers, testing the boundaries they set. The child wants choose his or her own food and clothing.
		The child is a cautious climber. He or she understands units of time, and has a sense of right and wrong. The child can remember and repeat five numbers in a row. Jokes are more complex now. The child can understand diagonal lines and diamond shapes. The adult first molars; 4 incisors come in at this time.
Jupiter trine	7.9 years	More expansion into the social arena occurs, with some degree of management of the social systems being encountered. The basis of one's moral or religious values is developed at this age. In addition, there develops the capacity to learn a new approach. A sense of fairness develops. There is an understanding of the difference between fantasy and reality.
		Note, many children have been watching cartoons and movies for years. Do not expect them to fully understand the difference between fantasy and reality before the age of seven or eight, even if you tell them.
Jupiter square	8.9 years	Here is a period of challenges. The child measures the results of actions, and the moral sense develops further. There may be a choice to be more oneself and less what others want. Another choice may include setting higher or different goals. A third choice is to contribute spiritually to the world. Social relationships need to reflect one's higher purose. The child uses irregular plurals (women, mice) more consistently.

Saturn trine	9.8 years	The child is able to remember strange faces. He or she is aware of bodily changes. The child collects things. The first pre-molars come in.
Jupiter sextile	9.9 years	Now there is an opportunity to "reconsider social ideas and goals." There is a chance to see what they really want for themselves and for friends. Children have the opportunity to seek new horizons in their thinking and actions. Group activities move them ahead in life.
Jupiter semisextile	10.9 years	Personal relationships undergo changes, and this is both painful and beneficial.
Jupiter conjunct	11.9 years	This is a time of coming of age ceremonies around the world. There is a transition to a more grown-up phase. Physically the onset of puberty is a key focus of attention. It is time to assimilate a larger biological and psychological consciousness. This is a time when habits can be changed. It is a time to take the initiative in the area of life where Jupiter resides in the birth chart. May have moral conflict. Feels capable and in control.
Saturn quincunx	12.3 years	Third molars (wisdom teeth); may or may not appear.

Neptune-Physical and Emotional Sensitivity

Neptune semisextile	13.7 years	Psychic ability may first emerge.
Uranus sextile	12 to 14 years	Sexual and emotional opportunities arise. Teens desire to reach out to form strong relationships with others.
Saturn opposition	14.7 years	A major shift from childhood to adulthood occurs here. The development of mental capabilities includes analytical thinking and critical evaluation of information. Teens at this age are more capable of abstract thought. Sexuality becomes an issue between child and parents. There may be rebellion, and the evading of responsibility for actions. Teens test the limits of behavior. They may move beyond their peer group attachments, as they no longer depend on their approval as much.

Saturn quincunx	17.2 years	Often the adjustment from high school student to some other role occurs around this time.
Saturn trine	19.6 years	A generally comfortable period during which one gains more education, either in formal schooling or in workplace or parenting roles.

Pluto: Extra-sensory Perception; Non-conformity; Power; Collective Consciousness

Pluto semisextile	12 to 31 years	Integrating emotions, thoughts, and spiritual values into a cohesive sense of self.
Uranus square		There is a mental crisis. Your sense of the future—your intuition—strives to see what is ahead, and you learn new ways of planning for the future.
Saturn square	22.2 years	Now there is a "crisis of consciousness." You are ending the period of dependence upon your parents. You can stand alone. You have mental individuality (yet you are not a hermit). There are many philosophical questions arising for you. You may have your first adult romantic relationship; that is, the first romantic relationship that is not based on some form of dependency.
Saturn sextile	24.1 years	Opportunities in social and career venues; growing patience and self-discipline, based on a sense of timing.
Saturn semisextile	27 years	
Neptune sextile	27.5 years	There is an unfocused approach to life at this time. You are able to replace the familiar surroundings, acquaintances, and ideas with less familiar experiences. There is a potential for expansion into new psychological territory.
Uranus trine	28 years	You become more conscious of your own ego and how it functions. There is greater intuitive development at this time.
Saturn conjunct	29.5 years	The person reaches out from the self; moving into the productive cycle; conclusion of the personal, physical developmental cycle.
Uranus quincunx	32 to 35 years.	
Neptune square	41.2 years	Along with Pluto and Uranus aspects (see below), the Neptune square issues in a period of

		potential doubt. You may feel you have not accomplished the goals you set for yourself, and you may feel disillusioned about your own potential. Inner conflict can lead to difficulties in relationships, but also the growth of compassion for yourself and others.
Pluto sextile	24 to 61 years	Opportunities abound for self-development in mental, emotional, and spiritual arenas. Possible opportunities to improve health or change one's appearance.
Uranus opposition	39 to 42 years	Psychological reorganization occurs. You find some success on the social level. The psychological upheaval relates to intimate relationship in the romantic, social, and/or professional spheres. This can be a confusing time, as you are changing your thinking on fundamental issues.
Uranus quincunx	47 to 49 years	
Neptune trine	54.9 years	Peak of spiritual expansion; opening to non-material side of existence. Transforming according to a more ideal but realistic self-image.
Uranus trine	54 to 56 years	You may have a resurgence (or beginning) of occult experiences. There is a sexual upheaval. For women this is the likely timing of menopause, although you may have felt it approaching for some time. For men it may be a time of rethinking your sexual activities. There is emotional conflict associated with these sexual changes. You may be seeking to reclaim your youth in some way.
Pluto square	38 to 86 years	Depending on the date of birth, the potential age range for this aspect is vast. Considering the power of this aspect of Pluto to the natal position, the difference in age can make a huge difference in the developmental path of the individual, and for the generations in which early or late transits occur.
		Challenges at this juncture include any transitions and the capacity to flow with them; increased or different involvement with groups, spiritual revitalization, increased clairvoyance or psychic awareness.

Uranus square	61 to 63 years	There is a theoretical chance for a third birth, associated with the second Saturn return and the Uranus square. You harvest the fruits of your past efforts. You are born into wisdom if your intuitive development has proceeded well. You now are able to teach what you have learned.
Neptune quincunx	68.6 years	
Uranus sextile	70 years	This is a period of extensive abstract thought, social fulfillment. You gain greater wisdom during this period.
Uranus semisextile	77 years	
Pluto trine	52 to 115 years	Note the tremendous range of ages here. You become more sensitive to global problems and develop a desire to draw on your internal resources, drop masks and facades, and open your heart to spiritual matters. New technology may capture your interest.
Neptune opposition	82.4 years	Resolution of false assumptions about the self; reversals of emotional attitude; self-illumination, if we begin to withdraw into our inner world in a state of serenity.
Uranus conjunct	84 years	You now reach a symbolic peak in your spiritual development. While you continue to learn and grow, you no longer feel constrained to maintain any particular social contracts. The inner journey becomes far more significant to you.
Neptune quincunx	96.1 years	
Pluto quincunx	65 to 140 years	
Neptune trine	109.9 years	Only a handful of individuals live to see this milestone.
Pluto opposition	85 - 160 years	If this aspect occurs within your lifetime, it will presage a period of time when you obtain a deeper perspective of your role in the social realm. You will learn to forgive others, if you have not already done so.

Appendix Two
Pluto Ingresses to Signs

Pluto Enters Sign	Year	Years to Square	Years to Opposition	Historical Figure's Birth Date
Leo	1447	43	85	1452 Da Vinci
Virgo	1464	38	88	1469 Machiavelli
				1473 Copernicus
Libra	1478	37	99	1483 Martin Luther
Scorpio	1490	42	116	1491 Henry VIII
				1493 Paracelsus
Sagittarius	1502	50	136	1503 Nostradamus
				1509 John Calvin
				1515 Teresa of Avila
Capricorn	1516	61	152	1523 Naibod
				1527 John Dee
				1530 Ivan the Terrible
Aquarius	1532	74	160	1533 Elizabeth I
				1535 Pope Gregory XIV
Pisces	1552	86	158	1564 Galileo
				1572 Kepler
				1574 Pope Innocent X
Aries	1577	99	147	1583 Morinus
				1599 Oliver Cromwell
				1602 Lilly

Taurus	1606	86	130	1608 John Milton
				1616 Culpeper
				1633 Spinoza
Gemini	1638	72	110	1643 Newton
				1656 Edmund Halley
Cancer	1668	56	94	1685 Bach
				1685 Handel
Leo	1692	44	85	1694 Voltaire
				1706 Ben Franklin
				1709 Samuel Johnson
Virgo	1710	38	87	1710 Giovanni Pergolesi
				1710 Louis XV
				1721 Madame Pompadour
Libra	1724	38	98	1724 Immanuel Kant
				1728 James Cook
				1735 John Adams
Scorpio	1736	41	115	1737 John Hancock
				1740 Marquis de Sade
				1743 Thomas Jefferson
				1743 Lavoisier
Sagittarius	1748	49	134	1749 Goethe
				1756 Mozart
				1757 William Blake
Capricorn	1762	60	150	1765 Eli Whitney
				1770 Wordsworth
				1770 Beethoven
				1775 Jane Austen
				1775 Charles Lamb
Aquarius	1777	74	160	1778 Lord Byron
				1786 Davy Crockett
				1792 Percy Shelley

Appendix Two/129

Pisces	1797	85	159	1797 Mary Shelley
				1797 Kaiser Wilhelm
				1801 Brigham Young
				1803 Emerson
				1804 George Sand
				1806 Saint Catherine
				1809 Darwin
				1809 Lincoln
				1809 Poe
				1817 Baha'U'llah
				1819 Queen Victoria
				1819 Walt Whitman
				1819 Herman Melville
Aries	1822	90	149	U. S. Grant
				1822 Louis Pasteur
				1835 Andrew Carnegie
				1835 Mark Twain
				1837 J. P. Morgan
Taurus	1851	86	132	1856 Freud
				1865 W. B. Yeats
				1875 C. G. Jung
				1877 Edgar Cayce
				1879 Einstein
Gemini	1882	74	113	1882 C. C. Zain
				1882 James Joyce
				1906 Arthur Young
				1911 Pope John XXIII
				1913 Richard Nixon
Cancer	1912	59	96	1913 Rosa Parks
				1918 Nelson Mandela
				1929 Martin Luther King Jr.
				1936 Michael Landon
				1936 Silvia Brown
				1936 Noel Tyl
				1937 Maggie Nalbandian
				1937 Colin Powell

Leo	1937	46	86	1937 H.H. Dalai Lama
				1937 Boris Spassky
				1937 Bill Cosby
				1939 Elizabeth Clare Prophet
				1939 Chogyam Trungpa
				1940 Mario and Aldo Andretti
				1940 Maria K. Simms
				1946 Stephen Erlewine
				1949 David Cochrane
				1955 Dodi Al Fayed
Virgo	1956	39	87	1956 Bill Gates
				1956 Steve Ford
				1956 Joe Montana
				1956 Tom Hanks
Libra	1971	37		1971 Koko the Gorilla
				1972 Bosenbecker Twins (Brazilian models)
				1982 Prince William
Scorpio	1983	40		1984 Prince Harry
				1985 H.H. Ögyen Trinley Dorje, the Karmapa
Sagittarius	1995	48		
Capricorn	2008	58		
Aquarius	2023	72		
Pisces	2043			

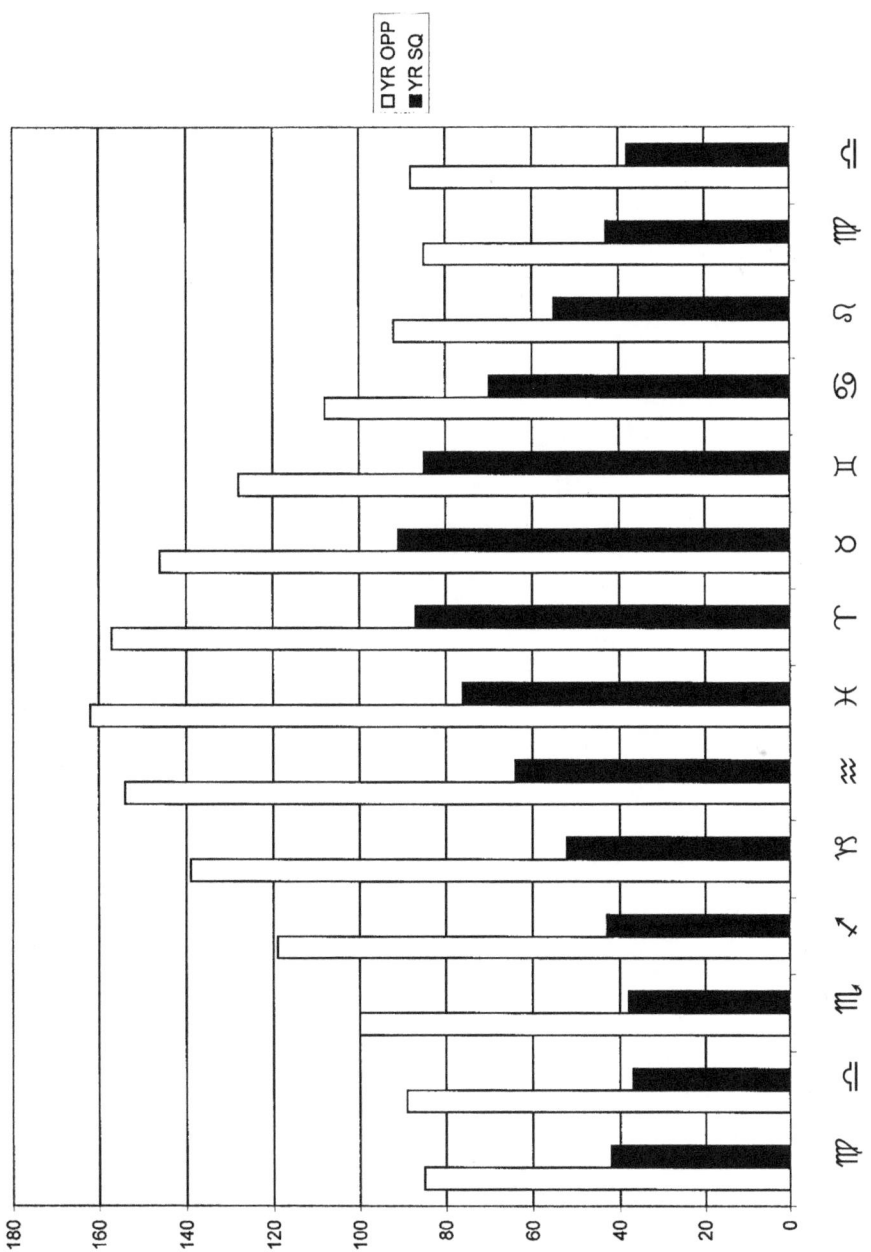

Years to Pluto Square or Opposition

Bibliography and Suggested Reading

AstroDatabank. AstroDatabank.com/NM/CobainKurtPRT.htm. (found on 04-09-2006)

Bailey, Alice. *Esoteric Astrology*. New York: Lucis Publishing Company, 1951.

Bailey, Alice. *Ponder on This*. New York: Lucis Publishing Company, 1971.

Burk, Kevin. *Astrology*. St. Paul, MN: Llewellyn, 2001.

Farnell, Kim. , "Astrology & the Young Child - Before the First Saturn Square, www.astrology-world.com/articles/farnell.html, accessed 8/29/2002

Gallup, Anderson, and Shillito. The Cognitive Animal," by Gallup, Anderson, and Shillito. Grimpeur.tamu.edu/-colin/TCA/Ch/Gallup/gallup-final.pdf. Read on March 26, 2006.

George, Llewellyn. *Llewellyn's A to Z Horoscope Maker and Interpreter*. St. Paul, MN: 2003.

Grell, Paul. *Keywords. Washington*: American Federation of Astrologers, 1970.

Healy, Jane M., Ph.D. *Your Child's Growing Mind*: *A Parent's Guide to Learning from Birth to Adolescence*. Garden City, NY: Doubleday, 1987

*Lansdown, Richard and Marjorie Walker. Your Child's Developm*ent from Birth through Adolescence. New York: Alfred Knopf, 1991.

Lundsted, Betty. *Planetary Cycles*. York Beach, ME: Samuel Weiser, 1984.

National Center for Health Statistics. "Infant Mortality," http://www.cdc.gov.nchs/fastats/infmort.html, 4/12/2002.

Ruperti, Alexander. *Cycles of Becoming*. Davis, CA: CRCS, 1978.

Sullivan, Erin. *Retrograde Planets Traversing the Inner Landscape*. New York: Penguin, 1992

Tierney, Bil. *Alive and Well with Neptune*. St. Paul, MN: Llewellyn, 1999.

Tierney, Bil. *Alive and Well with Pluto*. St. Paul, MN: Llewellyn, 1999.

Tierney, Bil. *Alive and Well with Uranus*. St. Paul, MN: Llewellyn, 1999.

Tyl, Noel. *Astrology and Personality: Astrological and Psychological Theories*. Saint Paul: Llewellyn, 1974.

Tyl, Noel. *Solar Arcs*. St. Paul, MN: Llewellyn, 2001.

Wikipedia, the free online encyclopedia.

Young, Arthur M. *Nested Time: An Astrological Autobiography*. Cambria, CA: Anodos Foundation, 2004.

Young, Arthur M.. *The Reflexive Universe: Evolution of consciousness*. Lake Oswego, OR: Robert Briggs Associates, 1990.

Young, Arthur M.. *The Geometry of Meaning*. Mill Valley, CA: Robert Briggs Associates, 1976.

Endnotes

[1] Healy, Jane M., Ph.D. *Your Child's Growing Mind: A Parent's Guide to Learning from Birth to Adolescence.* Garden City, NY: Doubleday, 1987, p. 32

[2] George, Llewellyn. *Llewellyn's New A to Z Horoscope Maker and Interpreter.* St. Paul, MN: Llewellyn, 2003, p. 247.

[3] Tyl, Noel. *Astrology and Personality.* Saint Paul, MN: Llewellyn, 1974, pp. 84 - 88.

[4] Burk, Kevin. *Astrology.* St. Paul, MN: Llewellyn, 2001, pp. 221-222.

[5] Ennis, Stephanie. *Twin Angles.* Evergreen, CO: 1978, p.10. (self published)

[6] Lansdown, *Richard and Marjorie Walker. Your Child's Development form birth through adol*escence. New York: Alfred Knopf, 1991, p. 127.

[7] Basic ideas for the first three progressed lunar aspects are taken from Kim Farnell, "Astrology & the Young Child, Before the First Saturn Square," www.astrology-world.com/articles/farnell.html, accessed 8/29/2002.

[8] There are numerous Internet sites that discuss the Jonas method in detail. I was unable to locate what I consider to be an original source of information about Dr. Jonas and his work.

[9] Ruperti, *Cycles of Becoming.* Davis, CA: CRCS, 1978, p. 81.

[10] "The Cognitive Animal," by Gallup, Anderson, and Shillito. Grimpeur.tamu.edu/-colin/TCA/Ch/Gallup/gallup-final.pdf. Read on March 26, 2006.

[11] Bailey, Alice. *Esoteric Astrology.* New York: Lucis Publishing Co., p. 126, 139, 171.

[12] Ruperti, Alexander. *Cycles of Becoming.* Davis, Calif.: CRCS, 1978.

[13] Ibid.

[14] from Wikipedia, the free online encyclopedia.

[15] http://encarta.msn.com/encyclopedia_761561931/Teeth.html, found 12/26/05.

[16] http://www.medical-library.net/sites/framer.html?/sites/_human_growth_hormone_(hgh).html (found 12/26/05

[17] Hennig, Lianne Olive. "Intuition." http://au.geocities.com/olivane44/intuition.htm

[18] Lundsted, Betty. *Planetary Cycles.* York Beach, ME: Samuel Weiser, 1984, p. 68.

[19] Ruperti, p. 212.

[20] Bailey, Alice. *Esoteric Astrology.* New York, Lucis Publishing Company, 1951, pp. 297-98.

[21] Tierney, Bil. *Alive and Well with Neptune*. St. Paul, MN: Llewellyn, 1999, p. 279.

[22] Ibid., p. 280.

[23] Ibid., p. 282.

[24] Reeves, Ricki. *The Quindecile*. St. Paul. MN: Llewellyn Publications, 2001, p. 188.

[25] AstroDatabank.com/NM/CobainKurtPRT,htm. (found on 04-09-2006)

[26] Ebertin, Reinhold. *The Combination of Stellar Influences*. Aalen, Germany: Ebertin Verlag, 1972, p.84.

[27] Tierney, *Alive and Well with Pluto*. St. Paul, MN: Llewellyn, 1999, p. 221.

[28] Tierney, *Alive and Well with Neptune*. St. Paul, MN: Llewellyn, 1999, p. 279.

[29] Ibid., p. 280.

[30] Tierney, *Pluto*. St. Paul, MN: Llewellyn, p. 222.

[31] Ibid., p. 223.

[32] Tierney, *Neptune*, p. 282.

[33] Tierney, *Uranus*, p. 266-267.

[34] Tierney, *Pluto*, pp. 224-225.

[35] http://en/wikipedia.org/wikiOlga_Korbut March 5, 2006.

[36] http://www.pbs.org/redfiles/sports/deep/sports_deep_bios_detail.htm.

www.ingramcontent.com/pod-product-compliance
Lightning Source LLC
Chambersburg PA
CBHW081839170426
43199CB00017B/2785